Ugh, stuff. Sometimes it feels like it deserves an "it's complicated" Facebook status. The struggle of having enough to feel comfortable and welcoming, but not so much that you feel suffocated and overwhelmed, is *real*. Which is why I devoured *Cozy Minimalist Home*. An approachable way to create a chic and inviting house that isn't stuffed to the gills so there's more room for life?! I'm in!

> —SHERRY PETERSIK, blogger, Young House Love; author,
> *New York Times* bestselling *Lovable Livable Home*

In her humorous, down-to-earth style, Myquillyn shows us how to stop trying so hard and instead create a space where we can exhale and simply be ourselves. Isn't that what home is all about?

> —LISA LEONARD, jewelry designer and writer

My home is my happy place, and it's even happier thanks to Myquillyn's encouragement, know-how, and practical guidance. She's taught me about decorating math, wall sabbaths, and personal style, and I adore the results I get to enjoy every day in my home. If you want to make your own home more warm, inviting, comforting, and welcoming, I highly recommend this book.

> —ANNE BOGEL, author, *I'd Rather Be Reading*

Here is what I love about Myquillyn and what I believe sets her most apart: she is primarily concerned with the way a space makes you *feel*. Her ultimate goal is to help people create spaces where people feel welcome, comfortable, cozy, relaxed, refreshed, and inspired. Contrary to a form-over-function culture, Myquillyn has developed a way to coach us into creating spaces where the people we love—and ourselves!—can feel our best. And lucky for us, she just happens to help us to make these spaces beautiful along the way.

> —LINDSAY SHERBONDY, owner and designer, Lindsay Letters

*Cozy Minimalist Home* puts to rest once and for all the assumption that minimalism needs to be cold, rigid, or impersonal. Quite the contrary—it is a life filled with passion, purpose, and beauty. Thank you, Myquillyn, for showing that to be true in this beautiful book and work of art.

> —JOSHUA BECKER, founder, Becoming Minimalist; author, *The More of Less*

I was hardly aware of the low-grade sense of failure I had every time I walked into my sunroom. And then I learned the Cozy Minimalist way and everything changed. Step by step, I applied Myquillyn's Cozy Minimalist method to my sunroom, and it went from being my least favorite room in the house to my most favorite within days. I'm so grateful for this beautiful, life-giving book.

> —EMILY P. FREEMAN, The Nester's little sister; author,
> *Wall Street Journal* bestselling *Simply Tuesday*

In *Cozy Minimalist Home*, Myquillyn explores what's missing from the minimalist versus hoarder conversation: in life and in decor, what does it mean to have enough? With an affirming approach, gentle guidance, and trusted tips, she's the grace-based KonMari we've been waiting for. Here's to more style and less stuff—within our own four walls and beyond.

> —ERIN LOECHNER, blogger, DesignforMankind.com; author; *Chasing Slow*

Myquillyn Smith's approach to living and decorating has inspired me for a decade. No home designer in America is better suited to speak to the everyday woman who craves beauty but doesn't have the time and energy for perfection. Her words and style have impacted my perspectives about design and have helped me transform my house into a home.

—JESSICA N. TURNER, author, bestselling books
*The Fringe Hours* and *Stretched Too Thin*

This is more than just a book about decorating; it is a manifesto. Myquillyn's down-to-earth, practical decorating advice and doable step-by-steps are what we house-lovers want. But it's her big-sisterly encouragement to use our homes to serve and gather and shelter and nurture that truly makes this book a must-read for anyone wanting their home to be a lovelier place.

—EMILY LEX, founder, Jones Design Company

Myquillyn elevates minimalism without sacrificing style, sets the stage for hospitality minus the production, and empowers even the most intimidated home decorator to make simple styling decisions that count. *Cozy Minimalist Home* will give you the freedom and confidence you need to simplify your style and make your house your own.

—RUTH CHOU SIMONS, artist; author, *GraceLaced* and
*Garden of Truth*; founder, gracelaced.com

Finally, a book that gives you permission to be minimalist *and* be cozy, to live with less *and* enjoy a beautiful home. If you think minimalism results in a cold, empty house, *Cozy Minimalist Home* will show you how to fill your home with what matters most to you and your family. This lovely book is as warm, cozy, and simple as you'll want your home to be.

—COURTNEY CARVER, author, *Soulful Simplicity*

When Myquillyn talks about home, I lean in and listen. She has a brilliance about her that makes it easy to forget that she's talking about home decor. I want her wisdom in so many areas of my life, but I'm happy to start with the living room. Strip away what's keeping you from serving people and then teach your rooms to do the same. This book is a gem and its author a rare gift to those who wish to make home a place of peace, love, and hospitality.

—EDIE WADSWORTH, author, *All the Pretty Things*

Step by step, chapter by chapter, Myquillyn writes as if she's your best friend who's moved in to destress your home *and* your life. With her "I've been there, and together we can do this" approach, you'll learn to curate a space with just the right balance. It's like clutter detox in a delightful interior-design book.

—KIM LEGGETT, author, *City Farmhouse Style*

Myquillyn is, no exaggeration, my go-to person for helping me reframe how I think about home. I'm a serial traveler, yet her enthusiasm for making my home a place I want to be keeps me grounded like few things I know. She's got a knack for mixing practical know-how with simple beauty, and her wisdom helps me actually love to hang up my backpack and start the tea—while loving everything around me. That's a tall order. I can't think of a person in my life who couldn't benefit from this book.

—TSH OXENREIDER, author, *At Home in the World*

# COZY MINIMALIST HOME

## ALSO BY
## MYQUILLYN SMITH

*The Nesting Place: It Doesn't Have
to Be Perfect to Be Beautiful*

# Cozy Minimalist Home

### More Style, Less Stuff

## MYQUILLYN SMITH

ZONDERVAN

*Cozy Minimalist Home*
Copyright © 2018 by Myquillyn Smith

Requests for information should be addressed to:
Zondervan, *3900 Sparks Dr. SE, Grand Rapids, Michigan 49546*

ISBN 978-0-310-35105-4 (ebook)

Library of Congress Cataloging-in-Publication Data

Names: Smith, Myquillyn, author.
Title: Cozy minimalist home : more style, less stuff / Myquillyn Smith.
Description: Grand Rapids, MI : Zondervan, [2018]
Identifiers: LCCN 2017056934 | ISBN 9780310350910 (hardcover)
Subjects: LCSH: Interior decoration—Amateurs' manuals. | House furnishings—Amateurs'
    manuals. | Minimal design.
Classification: LCC TX315 .S65 2018 | DDC 745.4—dc23 LC record available at https://lccn.loc
    .gov/2017056934

Published in association with literary agent Jenni Burke of D.C. Jacobson & Associates LLC,
an Author Management Company. www.dcjacobson.com.

*Cover design: Michelle Lenger*
*Cover calligraphy: © Lindsay Letters*
*Photography: Myquillyn Smith*
*Interior design: Kait Lamphere*

Second printing November 2018 / Printed in USA

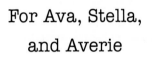

For Ava, Stella,
and Averie

Keep creating

# CONTENTS

To be human is to
long for home.

—JEN POLLOCK MICHEL,
*KEEPING PLACE*

Sometimes the questions
are complicated and the
answers are simple.

—DR. SEUSS

# INTRODUCTION

Your Style. Simplified.

It's August, and after years of renting houses and moving around, we just closed on our own home. A little white house with a green metal roof that sits on the edge of twelve acres now belongs to us. It's a complete fixer-upper. Every outdated surface, wallpapered wall, popcorned ceiling, tiny wood trim, and dark dusty corner is mine to make into whatever I want. I feel like the smartest person on earth to have grabbed up this inexpensive steal. How could we be so lucky?

*Five minutes later . . .*

It's still August, and after years of renting houses and moving around, we just closed on our own home. A little white house with a green metal roof that sits on the edge of twelve acres now belongs to us. It's a complete fixer-upper. Every outdated surface, wallpapered wall, popcorned ceiling, tiny wood trim, and dark dusty corner needs attention yesternow and will take one million dollars and every moment of my time to make right. I feel like the biggest idiot on earth to have grabbed up this pile of junk with a roof. How could we be so stupid?

And that's how I felt on a Monday within five minutes' time. It's now four years later, and every day I still feel both stupid and smart for buying this place.

## WHEN EMBRACING IMPERFECTION
## ISN'T THE ANSWER

Right before we moved into our little white house, I wrote an entire book about embracing the imperfect at home and in life, and if you haven't read it, you should. I wrote that book while living in a rental house after moving and living in a bunch of different homes for eight years. I completely believe that accepting the imperfect parts of life and sharing them opens up lines of connection with other people and is so valuable. Imperfections can work like magic fairy dust to help you let your guard down and let others in. Embracing imperfections and being content with where you are is an ideal first step to creating a home you love, but it's a lousy way to make design decisions.

Say you are having lunch with a friend. If you have spinach in your teeth and you know it, there's no amount of embracing imperfection that can solve your issue. Because no matter what, you aren't going to be comfortable with yourself until you get that spinach out, and neither is anyone else. You're not trying to look perfect, but you also don't want to look horrible and be a distraction.

Let's take it to the extreme. In your home, if you have no seating, no heating, and no drinking glasses you can use to serve guests, then you can tell yourself you are going to embrace that imperfection all day long, but the truth is you've got a problem that hinders you from using your home to the fullest. When you invite people over, you can't take care of them the way you want. You can't even take care of yourself the way you want. Being content with where you are makes you a lot happier, but it doesn't help you figure out why your home isn't working for you or understand why your room still doesn't look quite right. Just because we know perfection isn't the goal doesn't mean we don't long for—and need—function and beauty.

## MORE STYLE, LESS STUFF

So back to me and my fixer-upper. It was the first house we'd purchased in almost ten years, and also the smallest home we'd lived in for a while. And this time, I decided I wanted to do it "right." I wanted to approach this house with a clear mind and not get distracted by pretty throw rugs before it was time. And lucky for me, since I also write about my home online, I had an audience. I could no longer get away with endless temporary fixes and complaining about all the upgrades we weren't allowed to do because we were renting and those dumb landlords wouldn't even let us repaint a wall. Now *we* were the dumb landlords and the sky was the limit. Which meant everything was an option and I was suddenly overwhelmed.

I needed a logical approach to decorating that solved all sorts of issues. First, I needed to incorporate the stuff I already had. This is real life. There would be no buying all new furniture like they do on TV. I needed to decide where to focus a limited budget. And I desperately needed to free myself of the secret decorative hoard I'd been moving from house to house for years in

the hope of one day maybe possibly using it. Yep, all that time I was learning to find contentment in our rental homes, I was also saving up a two-car garageful of cheaply bought cute décor in case we might possibly need it in our forever home. When we moved to our new/old house, I had to store everything for a year in a glorified outbuilding where mouse and rust destroyed. I thought I was doing myself a favor by saving all that stuff, but in many ways I was making my life a lot more difficult than it needed to be, all in the name of being a good steward of thrifted finds.

There I was with a thousand design decisions to make, an audience watching, and a meager budget. I had a little white house just waiting to be made into a home and, finally, no landlord telling me what I wasn't allowed to change.

I needed a plan.

It's tempting to believe that finding your own style, giving it a clever name like Shabby Eclectic Steampunk Bungalow, and then searching those words on Pinterest will solve all your decorating problems. Ask me how I know that doesn't work. Instead, I realized that I needed to decide on my approach and then allow my style to come through from there.

I'm a busy mom with three teenage boys, a big hairy dog, and a husband who works outside and has twelve pairs of large dirty boots. I like pretty things, but not so much that they're allowed to make my life more complicated. I needed to know where to focus my time and money, what to keep and, above all, what to get rid of, all based on what I loved and how our family lived. I wanted, no, I *needed*, more style with less stuff, and along the way I realized less stuff gave way to more life.

I didn't have time to dust pretend plants, babysit delicate throw pillows, or stand guard over a pristine sofa. I needed a foolproof method I could trust to help me make decisions. Then I needed to apply it and be done enough to relax and finally use our home the way I'd always hoped.

But I also wanted all the pretty layers and storied goodness a well-lived-in home has to offer. Give me all the pillows and cushy throws, but watch out. I had some sort of internal threshold, and as quickly as I placed that last plump pillow on my sofa, the clouds cleared away from the full moon, my upper-lip bleach job faded away, and I got that crazed look in my eyes and declared that I wanted to burn it all down and keep every surface in our house empty from here on out. *Or else.*

I wanted, no, I *needed*,
more style with less stuff,
and along the way I realized
less stuff gave way to more life.

In reality, I longed for a home that allowed for messes like too many throw pillows, tons of boot storage, and a weird cat-puzzle collection, while still giving us some quiet, breathable spaces and the all-important cleared-off surfaces. I needed something that was part abundantly warm and welcoming, and part simple and no-fuss. And it had to be pretty. Listen, we all need to like our home so that we can use it to the fullest. Pretty is a must.

I started to pay attention to where I felt most inspired. I found myself reading blogs about minimalist design and noticing how relaxed I felt in spaces that had less stuff. But then I realized I read those blogs while snuggled up with my furry throw and fluffy pillows, both of which were lacking in those minimalist home photos I saw.

I was stuck in some awkward design space between cozy and minimalist. I was a Cozy Minimalist, a CoMi for short.

Just putting the words *cozy* and *minimalist* together felt like an accomplishment. For years, I felt a tiny twinge of guilt that I wasn't minimalist enough, that my ways were too complicated, that I needed to hire Marie Kondo to follow me around so she could kindly smack my wrist as I considered what to do next. At the same time, I was concerned that our home wasn't welcoming, warm, or cozily inviting. I had always felt like I needed to choose a side, but the problem was I saw the value in both sides. *Is there space in the design world for someone like me?*

I want to live in a world where there is room for plenty. Where meaningful collections are admired and loved and passed down through generations, where parties have oodles of hors d'oeuvres and piles of fruit and cheese on the platter. Where there is more than enough room for me to find a seat and get comfortable, and where I, in turn, share our abundance with others.

But I also love the invitation that a cleared-off surface offers, the freedom not to have to hang something on every wall just because it's blank, the discipline to know when to stop, and the reality that living with less makes my life so much easier. I wanted to remove distractions so I could truly see and, ultimately, so I could truly live.

I needed both the cozy and the minimal in my home, just like I saw it in the lives of the people and homes I admired most. Once I realized that I wanted

Once I realized that I wanted to be minimalist
in a cozy way and cozy in a minimalist way,
I was able to make real design decisions.

to be minimalist in a cozy way and cozy in a minimalist way, I was able to make real design decisions.

I'm a bundle of opposites, and I'm okay with that. I'm both smart and stupid for buying this house. I want both a filled-up and pared-down existence. I used to think this made me a crazy person; now I know this only makes me human.

I want to have just enough furniture and beauty in my home to serve my people and to get the style I'm after without overwhelming myself with stuff I have to take care of as a part-time job. I want to know where to focus my limited budget so it will have the most impact in creating the kind of home I want to provide for my family and friends without filling every nook and cranny just because space exists. I want the confidence to say "enough," no matter what the trends and salesclerks tell me. Even though I love a pretty home and a finished room, there are other ways I'd like to spend my time and money. I want to feel like my home is close to finished—probably not done, but done enough—where I'm free to part with my collection of stuff I was hoarding for Some Day.

Maybe you are drawn to the idea of more style and less stuff. You might be a Cozy Minimalist too without even realizing it.

## YEP, YOU CAN DO THIS

You don't have to be "designery" to finally make those design decisions for your home. Creating a home with a style you love isn't a result of some magical creative gene that you weren't born with. It's just a willingness to make informed decisions in the right order with a goal in mind. If you can make decisions, you can create a pretty house that isn't overwhelming. Creating a home you love is simply about deciding what to focus on and then giving yourself permission to stop worrying about the rest.

This book is all about helping you make house decisions using the filter of cozy minimalism. When you have clarity and purpose, you find motivation and confidence. You'd be surprised at how quickly things can change when you know where you're going.

This book is a *path*.

There is an order, and you can learn it and then apply it to every room of your home. You can't do it wrong if you do it right, and this book will show you how. Do not skip a chapter; do not work out of order. This is not the time to burn down your house, set all your stuff by the curb, or buy anything. I'll let you know if it comes to that. If you are ready to discover your style, simplified, you're in the right place.

Let's get your home looking the way you've always hoped so that you can use it the way you've always dreamed.

Let's get your home looking the way you've always hoped so that you can use it the way you've always dreamed.

I am overwhelmed by all
that has been given to me,
yet I seem to need more.

—CHRISTIE PURIFOY

# CHAPTER 1

# COZY

It Doesn't Have to Mean Cluttered

I'm gonna step on your toes in this chapter because I had to step on my own toes. And if I'm talking about toes, you know it's bad, because I hate feet. The goal of this book is to help you finish your house so you don't have to think about your house so you can live your one good life. But things might get worse before they get better.

Let's start with *cozy*, that little word we all love but might not know how to use. We've forced cozy into a job she was never meant to have. Until we realize that cozy isn't a style but a tool, we'll keep buying cute pillows and vases and not understand why we hate our rooms.

## COZY ABUNDANCE

It's autumn, and everywhere I turn I'm confronted with a new word I cannot pronounce. *Hygge*. It's Danish. It's an art. It's cozy. And everyone wants in on it.

You can try looking it up in the dictionary, but hygge is an essence or a vibe that's hard to describe with precision. It resists both tidy definition and accurate pronunciation by women like me who live in rural North Carolina. It's long been a way of life

*Hygge*. It's Danish. It's an art. It's cozy. And everyone wants in on it.

embraced by the Danes, who, for the record, are considered the happiest and most content people on earth. Hygge is all about setting the mood for coziness. Danes use more candles than anyone else, and this gives us a glimpse of one small way hygge works. Hygge is all about creating a cozy, safe, warm, and inviting atmosphere. It's about finding contentment and joy in the simple things like sitting by a fire playing a board game.

Here's the clincher: You are hygging all wrong if you are doing it alone. It actually requires people, otherwise it's not true hygge. Hygge is not a look or a style; it's an intention. The goal of hygge is cozy togetherness, get-through-it-ness, comfort, and knowing you are not alone. This is exactly how I want my house to feel no matter the season. Let's hygge!

I am irrevocably drawn to coziness, and if you are a human female between the ages of ten and 105, I bet you crave coziness too. It's everything I long for my home to be. But remember, in its best and purest form, coziness is a tool, not a style.

Cozy sets the mood for connection. It's inviting and warm, and it allows you to let your guard down. Cozy is your favorite jeans—not pretentious, not trying to be fancy, just comfortable in all the ways you need them to be. For most of my adult life, I've chased after coziness in creating a home for my family. No matter what style I was into, the cozy factor showed up in droves, preferably with cute bells on.

*Coziness feels like grace
and welcoming abundance.*

They say (heck, *I've* said) when it comes to creating a home, you should think of a few words that you want people to feel when they enter your home. And it also helps to think of a word that you do *not* want people to feel when they enter your home. Words I've always hoped people felt in my home are *connection, grace,* and *comfort.* And the one word I never want anyone to feel in my home? *Formal.*

To me, formalness requires you to be on your best behavior. This naturally puts the focus on how you act, which promotes focusing on yourself, which instantly kills all hope of true connection. I want the opposite of that, and for me that's always been comfort. I want a comfy place where everyone can just be themselves. One way to up the comfort factor is to create a cozy atmosphere. Coziness feels like grace and welcoming abundance, two things I value when it comes to our home.

But the only way I knew to create coziness was by filling my house with more and more stuff.

## COZY ABUSE

My entire adult life, I've been enamored with house and home and making beautiful things. Over the years, I've collected lots of pretty things, learned how to bargain shop for great furniture at low prices and then turn it into something usually really pretty—or sometimes horribly ugly, but that's all part of the fun. Somewhere along the line, this need turned into a hobby, and the hobby slowly turned into excess without my even noticing.

For the first twenty years of our marriage, Chad and I moved every few years, and the only way I knew to quickly create a home wherever we landed was to rely heavily on accessories like vases, candlesticks, figurines, seasonal décor, and pillows.

To me, adding style and coziness meant piling on more cute accessories. I thought cozy meant heaps, layers, and borderline overwhelm when it came

to stuff. I wanted all the fluffy pillows, soft throws, and candles. If we were renting and that particular home wasn't my style, I'd overcompensate by adding even more layers of stuff to draw attention away from the parts that weren't my style. In some ways, that's a great plan for anyone who moves around a lot and has a high need for coziness. But it comes with a price: the nonstop job of caring for lots of extra stuff and moving it from home to home. My dirty little secret was that my stuff was draining me. Slowly, my cozy overstuffed home was beginning to bring me less joy and more exhaustion.

One year, I learned how to sew just enough to be dangerous. I made pillow covers for every size pillow I could get my hands on, and then for some reason I thought it would be a good idea to organize every single one of those pillows on our bed in order of biggest to smallest. Our bed looked like a display in a pillow store whose owner was a hoarder but also had great taste. We had moved three times in two years, and I was longing for comfort and coziness, and maybe I felt like the more pillows I had piled on our bed, the more comfort

I could experience. They say it's smart to have a nightly bedtime routine, and every night Chad and I stood at the side of our bed like robots removing all the pillows and placing them out of harm's way in the corner of the room so we wouldn't trip on them if we needed to go to the bathroom or flee from the house if it caught fire. I'm pretty sure this is not the kind of bedtime routine they were talking about.

Having zero pillows on a bed or a sofa is uninviting. Keeping a few pillows on a bed or a sofa makes it just cozy enough to take a quick nap. Placing *every* pillow in a ten-mile radius on a sofa or bed results in needing to move things around before you sit down or take a nap, and suddenly, things shift from being cozifiers (thank you, Deborah Needleman, for that word) to stuff that's in your way. Your cozy stuff has now turned into a job. Instead of your stuff serving you, it's a source of frustration that moves from a pile on the bed to a pile you trip over on the floor. This is not cozy; this is a part-time unpaid job.

It has taken me years to figure out what I've always heard is true, that too much of a good thing can turn into a bad thing. I was doing cozy all wrong. Instead of serving people with coziness, I was abusing cozy.

Hello, my name is Myquillyn Smith and I'm a cozyholic. I'm addicted to the illusion of cozy, and I don't know when to stop.

## AN ACCIDENTAL STUFF MANAGER

In my years of collecting lots of cute stuff to make our house pretty and cozy, I had unofficially taken on another career. I was becoming a Stuff Manager, and here was my job description:

Look through stuff, put stuff away, organize stuff, feel guilty because I haven't organized other stuff, fuss at my kids because their stuff wasn't put away, wade through misplaced stuff in our garage, pile up stuff, pack away stuff, and move around stuff. Ask my husband where he put his stuff, and sort, wash, and dry all of that stuff.

Then I would dream about more stuff that I wanted and the bigger house I "needed" because my precious stuff wouldn't fit in our house—I guess it was too small.

I never planned on being a Stuff Manager; it just kind of happened, and then it became my job.

Oh, no, I didn't get paid for it. I just did it because I thought I had no other choice. I had a whole other job that I got paid for, and I used most of that money to buy more stuff. I trained my kids to be Stuff Managers too.

What? Why are you looking at me like that?

I made my life so much more difficult, all in the name of being cozy. I thought that a bunch of cozy stuff was what defined my style.

But remember, cozy isn't a style; it's a tool.

Moving to a smaller house made my addiction to cozifiers undeniable.

Cozy isn't a style; it's a tool.

Looking back, I'm really grateful we had to downsize, because at the time, I didn't realize what I was doing to myself.

Fifteen years ago, when our boys were little, we truly needed things. We needed desks for homework, extra seating for the family room, and artwork for the walls. I had a home without drapes, floors without rugs, and beds without bedspreads. We needed items for our home, and I learned how to find those things secondhand or on sale at a great price. This served our family well. We were able to furnish our home on a meager budget, our house was warm and inviting, and I had fun going out on the hunt.

The problem was, shopping secondhand and finding great deals became a habit, nay, a lifestyle. I didn't know when to stop. My thinking went something like this: *I can always work in an extra lamp—it's only thirty-nine dollars! What a deal! I'm paying cash and not going into debt. I am so smart! A well-made chair for a steal can always find a home with me; I'll worry about where to put it later. See how resourceful I am?! Look at all the money I'm saving as I buy inexpensive stuff at a discount!*

But was I really saving? I wasted time I didn't have thrifting, spent money on things we didn't need, and used gas to drive around to all the places thrifting required. I had to load and unload the item, usually with the help of some unsuspecting person, and then find a place for the item (usually a chair because I have chair addiction issues), resulting in moving other furniture around. I did all this to create a spot for something I didn't need in the first place. All in the name of cozy.

I didn't think about how everything I had in my home had a cost. I saw only the cost of not purchasing something. *What if I might need it? I can't pass up such a great find!* I neglected to count the cost of the time I spent shopping and transporting and finding a place for the things. I never considered that the money I spent on lots of smaller purchases could have been saved to make one quality purchase that I loved. And what about the time I'd spend caring for all my stuff and cleaning it (or most likely around it)? That was a cost I was committing to without realizing it. Not to mention the hidden cost of packing and transporting it in future moves. The most obvious yet somehow the most surprising part of all was this: filling up all the extra space in my home had a cost too.

## CLUTTER ANXIETY

Recent scientific research has shown that the level of cortisol—a stress-response hormone—rises in women when we are faced with the excess stuff in our homes. It's fascinating. The study reveals that this level doesn't change in men, only in women. Yep, clutter and chaos cause us to feel actual anxiety, stress, and even depression. I don't need a scientist in a white lab coat to convince me of the truth in that statement, and I'm guessing you don't either.

It's our job to find the right balance of cozy for our homes. Coziness and abundance can be inviting and warm, but too much stuff can be overwhelming and feel like a burden we were never meant to bear.

Moving to the smaller fixer-upper where we now live lowered my threshold for stuff. It didn't mean I liked stuff less or that I couldn't enjoy being in the homes of other people who had more stuff; it meant that I could no longer deal with so much stuff in my own home. Sometimes our stuff threshold is lowered by a health scare, a new baby, or a new job. It could also simply be the slow accumulation of things that finally catches up with us—an abundance of stuff loses its luster when it requires ongoing care and management.

If you are like me and are accumulating stuff without editing out other stuff, there will come a time when you will absolutely *have enough* of it. Suddenly, all that cute stuff that looks so good in everyone else's homes begins to feel oppressive to you. You've got extra chairs, extra lamps, and artwork that's still unframed and unhung. There are baskets full of random stuff, vignettes on every available surface, handed-down china collections, and holiday decorations that take up an entire section of the attic. All that stuff can quickly move from being potentially useful to being entirely too much.

I was busy making decisions about a fixer-upper and building a business. I didn't have time to baby all the cute items I owned or to carefully find the perfect spot to squeeze them into my home and life.

Our previous house had a garageful of just-in-case decorative items and furniture. We even had a pile of extra décor in the guest room. Not all of it was a waste. I had a vision of moving to a place where we could fix up a barn into a big gathering space—and that's exactly what we did. So lots of that stuff ended up being put to good use. But lots of it wasn't. If I was so good at finding great deals, why didn't I trust that I could find them a year or two later and not lug all that cute stuff with me from house to house?

Everyone's stuff threshold is different. My mom owns a lot of stuff and manages to keep it all under control. She can have collectibles and store stuff out on her counters. She can keep every meaningful item she wants, and it's all organized and cared for. She's able to locate things at a moment's notice because her house is spic-and-span and tidy. That has never been the case with me. For years I just thought I needed to be more organized. But then I realized I had a choice: either I could organize my ever-growing collection of stuff, or I could just have less stuff. Having less stuff sounded like the easy way out. And it is! But I don't want to get ahead of myself.

> Coziness and abundance can be inviting and warm, but too much stuff can be overwhelming and feel like a burden we were never meant to bear.

When I use cozy as a style instead of a tool, I end up feeling like I need more and more. It's a never-ending quest because I can always work in one extra pillow, and there's always a little surface still showing where I can pack in something pretty. I've fallen into the trap of collecting more stuff because a room felt off. I really believed if I could just add the right object, artwork, lamp, or chair, then my room would feel finished and I'd have that cozy style I was after. To me, decorating was all about *adding in* the right stuff. If I could just put the right things in the right spots, I'd love my house.

Sometimes it's possible to equate certain styles with excess stuff. For a long time, I was into the shabby farmhouse look. All the people I admired online who were also into that style seemed to have three times the amount of stuff in their house and on their surfaces than I had in my house. Instead of purchasing items I needed for my home, I was tempted to buy more and more stuff to make my farmhouse style look like the farmhouse styles I saw online, with their layers upon layers of beautiful things. Some people can do that and still keep a tidy house. I am not one of those people.

The truth is, no matter what style you love, you don't have to be a borderline hoarder to get it.

## WHEN THERE'S NO PURPOSE,
## COZINESS BECOMES CLUTTER

When I focus on cozy for people's sake, there's a stopping point. If I want a guest room to be cozy and inviting, I know it needs a warm blanket, something on the windows for privacy, some comfy pillows, and maybe a rug so our guests' bare feet don't land on a cold floor when they get out of bed. Either I have what's needed, or I don't. When I keep acquiring stuff because I can—without a goal—coziness turns into clutter, a distraction from the life I want to live. I'm assigning myself extra work to care for all of my precious stuff and, ultimately, that means my junk gets in the way of the people. People are the most important part of a home, not stuff.

When I focus on cozy for cozy's sake, I don't know when to stop. Then it doesn't take long for me to wonder why I'm surrounded by meaningless clutter that needs to be dusted and moved around so we can play a board game. Suddenly, my cute stuff is in my way, my house is messy, and I'm overwhelmed. I feel like I'm going to stuffocate because of all my adorable stuff.

## THE RIGHT WAY TO CREATE COZINESS
## IS ALWAYS TO KEEP THE PEOPLE IN MIND

Guess what? You and I are people too! Part of the job of cozy is to serve both us and other people in our home. Cozy's job is to make us comfortable, and real comfort leads to real connection. Coziness should serve us, not turn us into slaves.

When it was time to start making design decisions for our home, I did something really smart for all the wrong reasons. I created a Pinterest board for each room in my house. This is a good thing. After I had a bunch of pins for every room, I studied each board to see if there were any similarities. Also a good thing. I decided this would be a great way to figure out what color to paint my walls. One more good thing. And then maybe it would help me determine if there was a new kind of rug I should buy or more stuff I should get to help decorate my house. Hmm. Was that a good thing?

Cozy's job is to make us comfortable,
and real comfort leads to real connection.

After pinning rooms I was drawn to and then looking at them a few days later to see what they had in common, I was shocked. Almost every room I pinned had 75 percent less stuff in it than I had. But even more surprising was that all of the pinned rooms still felt abundantly cozy and inviting. Each room had all the important things, but most didn't have frivolous stuff all over the place like I had in my house. The rooms I loved were purposeful; every item in them had a voice—and the spaces were quiet enough that you could hear that voice. It was almost as if someone chose everything in the room to work together for a purpose. *Imagine that.*

This was a profound moment for me. For my entire adult life, I had focused on getting more stuff for my home in order to make it feel complete. Now I realized my problem might be that I had *too much* stuff—and none of the right stuff. Mostly it seemed I had the wrong stuff! I was my own worst enemy. My house was already exhausting me, and the only tool I had in my design arsenal was, "Buy more stuff, and then it will be better."

I'd thought I was a Minister of Coziness. Instead, I was just a Stuff Manager. I had been doing cozy all wrong.

This realization changed everything for me. I was tired of having so much stuff. I had all these pretty things, but my house still didn't feel right. I secretly longed for cleared-off surfaces, less pattern, and less stuff on the mantel. I needed to give myself the gift of less, but I wasn't willing to sacrifice comfort and coziness. But now I had hope. Could it be possible to use less in our home but still create that cozy feeling? And what about my own style? I love pretty things and want our home to represent our family. Was there a way to incorporate beauty and meaning in our home while using less stuff?

I was so afraid the only answer was to become one of those people who counts every item they own and despises throw pillows. There had to be some middle ground. I knew I was missing something. As it turns out, that something had nothing to do with more stuff.

That's all your house is, is a place to keep your stuff while you go out and get more stuff.

—GEORGE CARLIN

# CHAPTER 2

# MINIMAL

## It Doesn't Have to Mean Cold

I have been stereotyping minimalists for years. As much as I admired and respected those twentysomething bachelors who wore dark jeans and crisp white shirts and lived in their one-bedroom condos with only a sharp-edged black leather sofa and had no rugs and zero books, I just couldn't relate.

To me, minimal meant lacking and cold and modern. Minimal was barely adequate and sad. And I avoided it. I wanted plenty and abundance and coziness and warmth. *Give me all the layers and extras. Don't worry, I'll find an out-of-the-way place to stash them. And if we need a bigger house for it all, so be it!* When it came to creating a home, minimal seemed like the enemy of everything I held dear. So naturally, I assumed that minimalists wanted the kind of home that was the opposite of what I longed for. I looked down at my stereotyped minimalist bachelor with pity, but I also secretly envied him.

Meanwhile, life was happening. I had kids, moved a zillion times, and collected throw pillows with abandon. Then my cozy abundance of more stuff everywhere all the time started to feel like a burden. The boys would want to make a NASCAR track on the dining room table and I'd have to find a temporary home for the eight decorative objects (so stylish and thrifted at such a steal!) I had living there. Instead of housing sheets and towels, the linen closet was full of extra accessories I held on to in case I wanted to swap them out for a change of scenery. Things went in; nothing came out.

I looked around and realized we had closets packed full of great thrifted deals that I didn't have room for and stacks of chairs in our filled-up, carless two-car garage—you know, in case we ever moved and *might need* them in our next house. Oh, how the idea of maybe needing something tangled me up!

We'd move, and even though I hadn't used something for years, the smallest possibility that we might use it in the next house was enough reason for me to devote hours to packing and moving stuff we didn't need. I kept stuff out of fear. *What if I get rid of this when I might be able to use it later? What if I won't have enough? Look how responsible I am by keeping things I don't need—forever, just in case!* These were the early stages of a somewhat organized, really cute, bargain-bought hoard. And I'm messy to begin with.

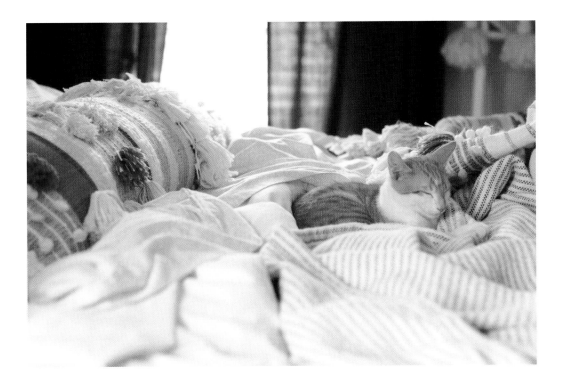

All my beloved stuff was stealing away chunks of my time and home and soul, and I was tired of it. I had a nagging feeling about it in our big rental house, but when we moved to a smaller house and I didn't have as many places to hide away all the stuff I'd been collecting, I could no longer ignore my problem. My cute stuff was in my way, even before I unpacked it, and I couldn't avoid it anymore.

But I'm still me and I still crave beauty and meaning. So how do I balance these things? How do I create meaningful beauty and an intentional home without going overboard by filling it with stuff?

Meanwhile, I started reading minimalist blogs. Some of them actually made me secretly jealous. The thought of owning less was a dream life I longed for. The freedom of keeping only what we truly needed, loved, and used sounded so extravagant and risky and glorious. But then I'd occasionally catch a glimpse of a minimalist home that scared me. As inviting as the minimalist movement was, some of these homes seemed like the opposite of inviting. There were no throw pillows, no rugs, no drapes. This was something I just couldn't commit to; a cozy home was too important to me. Cue the shopping bags.

And yet. Every now and then I fantasized about having a second, secret home. In this home, I would not have illicit affairs or hide a shopping addiction while I sat among piles of boxes from Home Shopping Network. No. In my wild, secret, second-home dreams, I envisioned myself as a minimalist. My secret second home would be gloriously empty except for a few well-thought-out pieces. In that home, I'd have the most comfortable, beautiful, nappable sofa with ideal pillow pairings. I'd have large rugs, big windows draped with pretty fabric, and no frivolous extra stuff to get in my way. There'd be a fireplace with a beautiful mantel, and the only thing on it would be some flowers I'd picked in the yard. Drawers would close easily and have extra space; surfaces would be empty, waiting to be used. My house would have just the right stuff and also be full of space.

Or sometimes I'd have a different fantasy. Our entire family, including the pets, would be away from the house, there would be some kind of natural disaster, and—poof!—our entire house would be destroyed—except, of course, our family photos and, miraculously, my favorite white sofa. We'd be forced to start fresh on our house, and this time I'd do it right without having to deal with all of our old crap.

My fantasy of becoming a private minimalist didn't seem likely. Wanting a second home so it could basically be empty was the craziest idea ever. And I'm embarrassed to admit that I've fantasized about our house being destroyed just so I didn't have to deal with a bunch of junk. I've also secretly wished I could have just one day in the county jail so I could simply read a book without interruption or stare at the wall and have meals delivered to my "room." I probably need to see a counselor. Or just rent a hotel room so my books and I can have some alone time.

Regardless, my view of minimalism slowly shifted. And I began to reconsider my definition of *enough*.

## THE ACCIDENTAL MINIMALIST HOME

In order to have some sanity in our fixer-upper while our kitchen was being demolished, I kept almost everything packed away in boxes, especially when it came to our family room, which is our family headquarters. I'd love to tell you that I did this on purpose, but I kept our family room sparse mostly because I was lazy and had no idea how I wanted to decorate the space.

*My view of minimalism slowly shifted. And I began to reconsider my definition of enough.*

For months we had only the essentials—places to sit, lighting, and a throw to snuggle under. It was so easy to keep clean! The emphasis was completely on the stuff we loved and used daily because I didn't have the bandwidth to deal with anything else. I started to appreciate walls with less stuff, the invitation of a cleared-off surface, and the quiet beauty of a home that had only what we needed. Having space in the house somehow magically translated into the feeling that I had space in my life. Breathing room on my walls, on my floors, and on my surfaces gave me breathing room in my life. I felt like I'd been holding my breath for years without realizing it, and now my simple home was like a big exhale I desperately needed. Home was a place I liked coming back to, a place that didn't demand more energy than I had.

Somehow my house became a quiet place even in the midst of remodeling. Isn't that crazy? Our home didn't even have a kitchen, we had temporary walls made of plastic and cardboard, all my beloved stuff was packed away, and yet, for the first time in a long time, home felt like a place of rest. Without excess stuff sitting around and needing to be managed, I could concentrate on all the stuff that really mattered, like family and friendships and life.

There is a way of being a minimalist that I can't get behind. It's having less stuff for less stuff's sake. A race to the least is just as meaningless as a race to the most. Only own four items of clothing? If there is a purpose to that beyond just having less, then great! But when there is no purpose, minimal is cold.

I started thinking about the word *minimal* in terms of purpose and came up with this definition: minimal is just enough to meet a goal. Why use more when you don't have to? Isn't that wasteful and troublesome? Instead of feeling like minimal was a punishment, I realized it could be a gift, both to myself and to everyone who lived in or visited our home. I had rejected the gift of simplicity for far too long, and now I was craving less. I wanted more and more of less.

> I had rejected the gift of simplicity for far too long, and now I was craving less.

Joshua Becker, author of the graceful minimalist book *The More of Less*, has the best definition of minimalism out there: "Minimalism is the intentional promotion of the things we most value and the removal of anything that distracts us from them." At its heart, according to Joshua, minimalism isn't about getting rid of stuff and doing without; it's about focusing on the right stuff.

We get to decide what stuff is important and give ourselves permission to get rid of the rest. This is something I can get behind! And it's something I experienced firsthand when I accidentally created a minimalist room in my house while we were renovating. I simply promoted the things I valued the most and didn't include the stuff that distracted me. Lo and behold, I *loved* it.

We're all probably tired of the William Morris quote, "Have nothing in your house that you do not know to be useful or believe to be beautiful." I'm tired of it myself. But I realized every time I read that quote, I mentally emphasized the words *useful* and *beautiful. Yep, got it, house stuff should equal useful and beautiful.* But I started to wonder if I'd been focusing on the wrong words in the sentence. Instead of *useful* and *beautiful*, what if I emphasized *you, know,* and *believe*? Who gets to decide if something is useful or beautiful? *You* and the people who live in the house get to decide—not your neighbor or the design blogger. And what if you are unsure? William Morris tells us, don't have it in your house unless you *know* and *believe* it's useful and beautiful. So if you think it might possibly be useful or beautiful in the *future*, then by William's standard, you're allowed to get rid of it. Freedom!

When our family room had less stuff, I was able to quickly clean up our house and make it guest-worthy in a matter of minutes. With less stuff, we could easily spot the things that were out of place. Homework didn't get lost in piles of old magazines and mail. The boys could keep track of their things, which made getting out of the house in the morning depend less on the divine intervention of a merciful God who had pity on us and more on a natural routine. And without all the cute little junk sitting around, I could see my stuff again. My ten-year-old slipcovered sofa held its own and still looked good with just a few pretty pillows. For the first time in ages, I noticed the pattern on our rug. Grocery-store flowers on the mantel had a much bigger impact when they weren't competing for attention with a thousand other tchotchkes in the room.

Everything in the room had presence and breathing room around it, and I loved it. Visually, we had some white space, and that had a profound effect on how I felt when I entered the room. Home was becoming less a chaotic place in my life and more a place of peace. Minimalism was the happiest accident I'd ever stumbled into, and I decided I had to have it in every room of my house.

## MINIMAL ISN'T A STYLE, IT'S A TOOL

Minimalism was just as valuable a gift to me and others as coziness. Wouldn't it be incredible if these two seemingly opposite design tools could work together to help us create the home we've always longed for?

Living in a fixer-upper while fixing her up might have been the best thing to ever happen to my decorating sense. For the first time in my life,

In the same way that we need a rest or a Sabbath every week to help us slow down, focus on what's important, and reconnect with God and those we love, what if we gave our eyes a visual Sabbath at home?

I longed for less because I really believed it was the easiest way to get the home I wanted.

But there was a downside. I knew I liked having less stuff, but I also had all this extra stuff I liked. How was a person like me, with my hoard of cute stuff, supposed to figure out what to get rid of?

I had to remind myself that the joy of having a house that served my family outweighed the pain of letting go of my cute stuff. All this time, I'd been doing things backward. I was keeping things in case they might possibly be useful or beautiful later rather than deciding what was useful and beautiful now. For too long, my actions had declared that keeping stuff for possible future use was more important than having a workable, easy-to-maintain home now. I wouldn't have ever said that, but that's what my behavior proved. Now I was confident that if I could get my house the way I wanted it, I wouldn't care about the stuff I had to get rid of. In her book *The Joy of Less*, Francine Jay says, "To be useful, an item must be used." Apparently, when it comes to stuff, it's useful only if you use it. Logic for the win!

I've stopped bringing things into my house just because they're pretty and a bargain. Stuff has to earn its keep so I can stay underwhelmed at home. I need to clear my house of visual clutter so I can have some breathing room. In the same way that we need a rest or a Sabbath every week to help us slow down, focus on what's important, and reconnect with God and those we love, what if we gave our eyes a visual Sabbath at home? For my entire decorating life, I've been putting too much focus on cozy and not giving enough credit to the power of margin and visual white space.

Bottom line? I've been missing one of the most important skills of good design: editing.

## YOUR NEW JOB DESCRIPTION

Instead of being a Stuff Manager, start thinking of yourself as Chief Home Curator. A curator is the protector of what comes in and what goes out. It's an important part of making home that we often forget about because buying new pillows is more fun than being mindful of how much stuff has come into our home.

A curator always keeps in mind the overall goal and purpose of a space. She knows there are many good and beautiful things that can be included in a space, but she always keeps the interests of her people at the forefront when making her choices. That's all design is—making rational, informed decisions about the best things to use in your home based on your needs and personal preferences.

We need homes that truly serve us and our families, homes that look the way we want them to look so we can use them the way we feel called to use them. We need homes that are both cozy and minimalist in all the right ways.

Once my kitchen renovation was complete, I lost my flimsy excuses for not unpacking. It was time to settle in and make decisions about how to decorate this house in a way that served us, looked good, and helped us to welcome and serve others. It's one thing to cheer on minimalist ways as a

> Less stuff not only
> simplifies my home but
> also simplifies my life.

survival strategy when you've just moved into a home; it's another thing to choose minimalism as a lifestyle. The thing that keeps me going now is that I'm convinced less stuff not only simplifies my home but also simplifies my life. I refuse to let go of that wonderful feeling I had when I first experienced having less stuff in my house.

Margin in my home is just as valuable as a great sofa. My ongoing goal is to create a home that I love, that works for my family, and that uses just the right amount of stuff and not a thing more. It doesn't mean I'm in a race with myself to have empty walls, and it doesn't mean I won't ever buy anything for my home. It simply means I'm going to focus on using and buying the right stuff with purpose.

If you are with me and are ready for your home to be a place that truly welcomes you at the end of the day, that represents your family, that helps you live the life you've always wanted instead of getting in your way and demanding all your attention, then you are a Cozy Minimalist too. CoMis unite! Let's face home head-on and make smart design decisions that serve us well in all the right ways.

As a Cozy Minimalist, you'll finally get that cozy style you long for using just the right amount of stuff. Not a thing more. Your home will be a calm place of rest, not an eyesore that demands your constant attention. Home is never "finished," because families are always changing. But that doesn't mean your home has to look like you're living in a never-ending DIY project. You'll finally get to a place where tweaking your home to serve you better is a quiet joy, not a mess you keep tripping over.

I'll help you decide what does and doesn't work for your home based on your family's unique needs. I'm going to walk you through a method that will help you get your home looking the way you've always hoped so you are free to release those things that are weighing you down.

Since becoming a CoMi, I hardly even think about my house. It looks great, it functions just the way we need it to, it's flexible, and I like being there and having guests. I knew something profound had changed when I could invite people over and focus on connecting with them rather than being preoccupied with how my house looked. This is what being a CoMi can do for you. My house works for me, it serves me well, and I enjoy it. I just had to learn how to make the right decisions to help it do all of that.

It starts by knowing where *not* to start. Let's do this.

If a home doesn't make sense, nothing does.

—HENRIETTA RIPPERGER

# CHAPTER 3

# THE MYTH
# OF FINDING YOUR
# SIGNATURE STYLE

You Already Know What You Like

I can't pass up a chance to take one of those "find your perfect style" quizzes, and I bet you can't either. Why? Because we think if we could just define our style, then our decorating decisions would be so easy. We'd love to have an irresistible style name like Chunky Vintage Cottage Glam, or Southern Traditional Primal, or even Mid Mod with a pinch of Mountain Man. We think if only we knew what our *style* was, then we could solve our problems, and our house would look and feel right.

*Wrong.*

I've never been good at defining my style, and the few times I have tried, it still didn't help me make decisions. There are no stores devoted to French Coastal Rustic Vintage Farmhouse or Tropical Midcentury Boho with a touch of Industrial. Even if you had the perfect name for your style, you'd still have to make decisions about everything you bring into your home, not to mention how those things relate to all your other stuff. Decorating can be fun, but that doesn't mean it's easy. We are using up real money, real time, and real square footage. Finding a cute name for the style you love sounds fun, but it doesn't solve any real problems or help you know what you should or shouldn't use in your house.

I wish this book could have a chapter that detailed ten cute styles with fun names and step-by-step instructions for how to get each style so your home looks great and you never have to clean it again. The problem is, I don't believe in that junk. It's just not that easy. Unless you want to live on the set of *Mad Men* or *The Truman Show*, no one wants to fully embrace one particular style—this is exactly what makes creating a unique home equally wonderful and difficult. Add together the stuff you already own, the unique style of your house, and your family's needs, and there's clearly no formula that could ever work.

## WHAT WE REALLY WANT

Now that I've decided I'm going to be a Cozy Minimalist, I'm realizing that there are two things just as important to me as having a cute, stylish house: function and simplicity. I could have the prettiest home in the world, but if it doesn't have enough beds for my family, all that prettiness is useless. Joanna Gaines could design the cutest house in town, but if it didn't have a bathroom, we couldn't live in the house. I could own every pretty thing I've ever come across in my life, but that wouldn't make my life better; it would just make it overwhelming.

What is it we really want out of our homes, and how do we know when we've got it?

Most of us want to feel good about our home. We want to like being there, to feel content in our rooms, and to love the way they look and feel. But maybe admitting that feels risky to you. Maybe you think it's somehow sacrilegious to feel good about your home. You equate loving your home with pride and materialism. Stop thinking like this.

Let me ask you this: When you don't love your home, how does it affect you? Does it cause you to hesitate about or put off having people over? Are you able to rest, focus on others, and be truly attentive in your home if you are preoccupied with your feelings about where you live? Most of us long to create a home not so that it can be featured on HGTV, but so that we can fully use, love, and enjoy it.

We long to create because we were made by a creator. In her book *A Million Little Ways*, Emily P. Freeman makes a simple yet profound observation: "The first thing we know about God is that he made art. What is the first thing we know about people? We were made in the image of God." In the beginning, *God created*. As humans created in his image, we are naturally creative beings, whether we admit it or not. Not only do we have the urge to create, but when we step back and look at the story of what God is doing, we see something that explains why we long to create home. Author Jen Pollock Michel writes, "In the beginning of time, God made a home for his people and at the end of time God will make a home for us." She goes on to point out that our first home was in a garden, and our last home will be in a city.

God is in the business of creating places for his people. He is the original homemaker. So here we are in the gap somewhere between the garden and the city. It's no wonder we sense that making home is an important calling. We were made to crave beauty. We were made to crave home. That's not a bad thing! Let's move forward with creative purpose to make a home that serves us well, so that we, in turn, can welcome and serve others well.

## FIND YOUR STYLE BY PAYING ATTENTION

Instead of wasting your time trying to name your style, start honing your design skills by learning how to pay attention. The entire world is a design classroom if you're willing to see it that way. Every room you walk into and every photo of a room you see can teach you something. You can learn just as much from rooms you hate as you can from rooms you love. Sometimes more! You just need to become a student of your surroundings and then ask yourself a few questions:

- What about this room draws me in?
- What works for me?
- What do I love about this space?
- What ideas can I steal for my own use?
- What do I dislike about this room?
- How does this room make me feel? Do I feel safe, nervous, calm, annoyed, etc.?
- Why does this room make me feel the way I do?
- What design risks or unexpected elements are evident in this room?
- What might hold me back from creating a room like this? Why?

Answering questions like these will help you recognize mistakes you might be making in your own home. Sometimes it's easier to see them first in a space that's not your own.

Look at furniture placement, patterns, scale, unique ideas, pairings, focal pieces, plants, windows, details, proximity of pieces to one another, lighting, texture, negative space, art, and storage pieces. You are a room detective, and this is the most fun job ever! When it comes to fulfilling your duties as Chief Home Curator, at least half your job is simply to pay attention. That's something you can do in every room on earth—from the dentist's office to the hotel lobby, from your mom's house to the restaurant where you ate lunch. *Pay attention.* What's working for you? What's not working for you? How can you translate what you observe and apply what you learn to your own home?

This can be as simple as paying attention to how you respond to certain environments. If every time you go to the dentist's office, you find yourself going around the waiting room and opening the blinds so you don't feel cooped up, you probably have a high need for natural light and light colors. Are you making the most out of your own natural light at home?

You can apply this to the people in your immediate family too. Maybe you notice that when you visit the home of a friend who has an abundance of toys, your child gets overwhelmed and excited to the point of exhaustion. But when you visit your mom's house with its single bin full of favorite toys, playtime is creative and sane.

Paying attention to how you respond to different spaces will help you realize what kind of atmosphere you need and enjoy in your home. When you

> When it comes to fulfilling your duties as Chief Home Curator, at least half your job is simply to pay attention.

pair this information with what you learn in the next section, you'll be able to make design decisions with more confidence, based on logic and observation not a few fancy adjectives that try to capture your personal style.

## FIND YOUR STYLE BY GATHERING INSPIRATION

Gathering inspiration is another way to hone in on your personal style. When you collect inspiration and see repeating themes and ideas, you'll begin to have more confidence in recognizing what you really like. But before you start collecting ideas, I want you to consider your method and your mindset. It's important that you gather both *purpose*-based inspiration and *passion*-based inspiration.

I'm going to use Pinterest as an example, but the same principles and process apply to ripping out pages from a magazine, using your phone to take photos from your favorite design book, or whatever new and improved way of collecting design ideas the world has come up with by the time you are reading these words. Say it's the middle of November, and you are going to be hosting Thanksgiving at your house. You're in charge of the turkey and stuffing, but you've never made turkey and stuffing by yourself. What do you do? You go to Pinterest, and you search with great purpose for the most delicious yet simplest recipe (which no one will realize was simple) with ingredients you can pronounce and find at your grocery store. You pin deliberately by saving only those options that might actually work for you. You mean business; you are looking for solutions, and nothing can get you off course. This is pinning with purpose.

Now say it's a Saturday morning and you have some time to yourself. The kids are all at Grandma's, your husband is out of town, you've just heated up some leftover coffee, and you have hours to do whatever you want. You end up on Pinterest, pinning any meal that looks like something that you might someday want to make and eat—no real purpose here. This is for your own enjoyment. You just want to have a place to collect all these different scrumptious-looking foods, no matter the ingredients or skill level required to make them. This is pinning with passion.

You need both of these gathering methods when it comes to figuring out your style. You probably already allow yourself to pin with purpose. For example, if you're looking for a rug, you might pin rooms with affordable rugs you don't hate, that will work in your living room, that you're sure you can find today at the store down the street, and that require little to no risk. You'll end up pinning some nice rugs, yes. But really, you would learn a lot more about the kind of rug style you loved if you'd just let yourself pin entire rooms you are drawn to and then go back and look at what those rooms and their rugs have in common. You might find you are putting way too much emphasis on the exact kind of rug you should get, when really, it's the room as a whole that makes or breaks whether you like it.

We tend to put lots of pressure on individual items in a room, failing to think about the finished whole of the room. Pinning with passion helps us see past this because we don't have to analyze every part; we just pin something because we love it. When we pin with passion, we don't have to explain why we chose something or feel confident we can recreate every detail.

We tend to avoid this kind of pinning because we think it's a waste of time. But it's not.

## PINNING WITH PASSION HAS GREAT VALUE

Sometimes people get too critical about their pins. They think they can't pin a room unless they 100 percent love everything in it, unless it's possible for them to copy every detail. No. Stop. This is not what you want to do. You will never love every single item in a room that you see somewhere else. It's good to learn from rooms and people that we don't 100 percent agree with. Because in reality, there is no room or person we will 100 percent agree with.

Allow yourself to pin with passion. And since you are reading this in the future, and there's probably some other amazing app to use now, whatever it is, use it with passion and abandon!

To create your Cozy Minimalist home, first simply collect images of rooms you love, organizing them by each room in your house. Yep, you want a separate file or pin board or other collection of ideas for every room in your house. Ideally, you will do this over time, but if you know you need to work on the family room, schedule thirty minutes every day for a few days, make a Pinterest board for that particular room, and start searching for rooms that you love and that feel right for your family room. Pin them all! This is not the time to evaluate whether the wall color would look good in your house or to eliminate a pin because you don't have a fireplace. This is a practice in allowing your personal style to reveal itself to you. Moving in a few months? You are so lucky; you get to focus on collecting inspiration for your next house before you even move in. Do not underestimate the importance of this part of the process. You will return to these boards for inspiration over and over as you cozy-minimalize your spaces.

## THE UNSELFISH ART OF BEING INSPIRED

I've received the lovely Ballard Designs catalog for almost fifteen years. And probably much to Ballard's dismay, I have never actually purchased one thing from them. But I don't email the Ballard people to tell them I no longer want their catalog or that they should change it because most of the things

*Inspiration is everywhere for the taking.*
*Take some and pass it on.*

in it are well beyond my price range and are not my exact style. No. If I expect inspiration to lead me to create a replica, then I don't truly understand the role inspiration plays in my life.

Inspiration is my responsibility. I go looking for it with purpose, and I hope to be open to any inspiration that comes my way. I also get to decide what inspires me. I don't judge the designer who pays a million dollars for a new coffee table or resent that person for having expensive taste I could never afford. That's what happens when you are looking for things to copy instead of looking for inspiration.

If I like something I can't have, I can choose to be jealous, resentful, or judgy, but I would miss an opportunity. The alternative is to get excited about the inspiration the thing I can't have provides. When I see that dreamy million-dollar coffee table, I start thinking about how I can create the same thing for forty dollars and then give myself a high five. Or, if I hate it, I roll my eyes at it and move on. I'm always on the hunt for inspiration. It goes like this: I pay attention to things I like, and then I ask myself how I can integrate those things into my own home. See how I turn everything around and make it about me? That's the secret of being inspired! It sounds selfish, but it's not.

Inspiration is everywhere for the taking. Take some and pass it on.

## YOUR PINTEREST READING

Now you are ready for a Pinterest reading. A Pinterest reading is similar to a palm reading, but minus the creepy fortune teller, the crystal ball, and the loss of your hard-earned money to a scam. All you need for a Pinterest reading are a few friends (it helps if you admire their homes), a little time, and fifty to a hundred images you pinned with passion with one space in mind.

Once three or four friends have agreed to read your Pinterest board, you can hang out together in person or just send them the link to your board. Ask your friends to look through your photos and write down what they notice about them. You can do the same for them. Here's what I learned from one of my first Pinterest readings:

- I pinned lots of circles.
- I was drawn to pink.
- I was clearly fond of white walls.
- Flowers and texture were important to me.

This information was really useful. I hadn't noticed any of that stuff in my pins, but at the same time, it wasn't surprising. Of course I like the color pink! I knew that; I just never gave myself permission to use it in my home.

Your Pinterest reading will be proof to yourself of the things you are drawn to, and you'll be reminded that, *yes*, you already know what you like! Now the fun part starts: How do you work those things into your home?

## FUNCTIONAL, ABUNDANT, BEAUTIFUL, AND SIMPLE (FABS FOR SHORT!)

If our goal isn't to mimic a style with an impressive name, what exactly are we trying to accomplish with the things we put in our homes? As Cozy Minimalists who want more style with less stuff, we'll use cozy and minimal as tools to create a home that is functional, abundant, beautiful, and simple. That's it. If we can incorporate those four traits into every space in our homes, our homes will serve us exceedingly well.

FUNCTIONAL. A CoMi knows that if her house isn't useful, then it's useless. First, she assesses the function of her spaces, and then she makes sure the cozy enhances the function and never hinders it.

ABUNDANT. A CoMi's home is warm, inviting, comforting, and welcoming. A CoMi realizes that small areas of abundance play a big part in helping her experience all those fuzzy feels that we call cozy. She uses pockets of abundance as a tool to cozy up her home. No matter what style she's drawn to, she gets to choose and adjust the threshold of abundance in her home.

BEAUTIFUL. A CoMi realizes the difference between beauty and perfection. She believes that her home doesn't have to be perfect to be beautiful. (See my first book, *The Nesting Place: It Doesn't Have to Be Perfect to Be Beautiful*.)

SIMPLE. A CoMi commits to more simplicity in her home because she understands that it makes her life easier without threatening her comfort level. She gets to choose and adjust her threshold of simplicity no matter what style she's drawn to.

You are your own house whisperer, and you need four ingredients to create a Cozy Minimalist home: simplicity and abundance, function and beauty. You don't need a style quiz to tell you what you like—you are already great at knowing what you like. You just need to learn how to incorporate what you already like into your home.

You are your own house whisperer, and you need four ingredients to create a Cozy Minimalist home: simplicity and abundance, function and beauty.

## BALANCE MAGIC

Years ago, we lived for a short time in a house built in the 1800s. It had dark wood floors, heavy moldings, and five coal-burning fireplaces complete with ornate iron covers and columns. Some of the rooms were wallpapered; others were painted deep colors. There were huge windows, twelve-foot ceilings, and vintage light fixtures. The kitchen had an orange Formica counter, dark brown cabinets, and yellow walls. There was a *lot* going on in that house. Even when it was empty, it had style and personality and presence. It wasn't necessarily *my* style, but it was style nonetheless.

After six months, we moved from this old beauty/nightmare to a brand-new little apartment. The apartment had eight-foot ceilings, beige carpet, beige walls, beige counters, and neutral everything. This place was born without style, but that didn't make it bad. It just meant I was starting with a blank canvas. The first thing I noticed when we moved in our circa-1940 dark wooden dressers was that I could see them again. In our previous house, they were swallowed up by the ceiling, detailing, and style of the house. Now that we were living in a beige box, everything suddenly had presence. I didn't have to work so hard to offset a style I wasn't in love with or even balance out a style I liked. I appreciated everything in the 1800s house; I just didn't want to feel like I was living in the 1800s.

Moving into that beige apartment allowed my 1940s dressers to have a voice again. Because they were no longer competing with their surroundings, they looked tailored and focused instead of like a bunch of vintage stuff in a vintage house. That was when I began to learn about the power of opposites and the secret of balance.

If you have a collection of ornate furniture, it will stand out best in a simpler room. If you have lots of clean-lined, modern furniture, it can look really great in an older house full of style, details, and character. Having lots of old stuff in an old house made my style feel frumpy and old-fashioned, but I couldn't figure out why until I saw all my stuff against the calm, quiet backdrop of a builder-grade apartment. Suddenly, my vintage dressers felt like a purposeful choice because they popped against the quiet beige wall.

It's all about creating balance. I bet you have a favorite pair of jeans. I'm willing to guess you also have a denim shirt. Maybe you even have a pair of cowboy boots. And over the last few years, you may have picked up one of those large-brimmed hats that seems to be in every store. Each of those items on its own can look great. But if you wear them together, you'd probably feel like you were wearing a costume. So most of us choose to wear the boots with a modern skirt instead of the cowboy outfit. Unless we are cowboys, we probably don't care to look like them, but that doesn't mean we can't use and enjoy the individual parts of the outfit.

The same principle applies when it comes to designing our homes.

It's easy to focus so much on one style that, before you know it, your home looks like a store where they sell chippy furniture. Or a store where they sell modern furniture. Or the set of a 1930s romantic movie. Or just plain weird.

You don't want your house to look like a store or a movie set. You want it to look interesting and pulled together with intention. We are individuals, and we each have a style, which is why there's not a magic design formula that works for everyone. But if you learn the subtle art of balance and apply it to your home, you won't need a formula.

Our home has twelve-inch-wide pine plank floors, a bathroom with cedar walls, a wooden mantel with raw edges, and a green metal roof. When we look

out the windows, we see trees, a pasture, or a broken-down sawmill. The trim is simple, and the overall feeling of the home in its naked state is rustic and country, with a tiny touch of cottage.

I love all of these characteristics, but they are heavy on country.

Since I don't want to feel like I live in a Cracker Barrel store, I'm careful about what I put in my house. It takes only a few pieces to make my house feel overly country and rustic. Even though I like those looks, I know that for my home to feel intentional, it needs to be balanced. In order to balance out the country-rustic-ness of this house, I simply needed to add some of the opposite. For me, the opposite of country is modern. So I decided to add a touch of modern. How fun is that? I've never been much of a modern fan, but my cottage style mixed with the country feel of the house was too rustic for me, and the only way to fix that was to add some modern. See, it's decorating math! Too much of one thing can be balanced out by adding a little of the opposite.

But I'm still me, so I added modern pieces I liked rather than forcing myself to choose something I hated just for the sake of balance. That meant going with pure white quartz counters with square edges to offset the country look of the kitchen. We bought a glossy, modern table with simple lines to balance out the expanse of rustic pine floors, and sprinkled around the house some extra chairs that have a modern feel. These touches of modern allow the rustic parts to have more presence and purpose because, together, they communicate conscious decisions I had to make. And that's why it feels purposeful.

I didn't add some modern elements because I changed my style. *Oh, now the Nester is a modernist, or whatever they are called!* No. It's because I moved and realized what this new house was asking for. Because I've honed my paying attention skills, I had my ears trained to listen to what my house was saying to me. I gave it a chance to tell me what it needed and listened attentively. We'll talk more about listening to your house in chapter 5. For now, just know my house was yelling COUNTRY, so I countered and turned down the volume with some touches of modern.

Have you ever been in a house in which each item looked well chosen and well placed? That's a pulled-together look. You can do that too! You just have to consider the overall feel of a room and incorporate some opposites.

- If a room is feminine, add some masculine.
- Too many florals? Add some wood or leather or plaid.
- If a room is traditional, add something funky and unexpected.
- If a room is light, add some dark contrast.
- Chippy, add some modern.
- Cutesy, add something mature.
- Patterned, add some white space.
- Slick, add some texture.
- Perfect, add something purposely imperfect.

Do you want to love your home? Stop decorating like someone else. The very thing holding back your space might be something you never chose in the first place, like that hand-me-down cabinet, the collection Aunt Margaret decided to start for you, or the sofa your husband picked out because it had built-in cup holders. When you are a Cozy Minimalist, you define your dream house differently than other people. You don't need marble counters, a walk-in pantry, or waterfalls in your pool. Not that there's anything wrong with those things. In fact, I would love to have all of those things, but I know I don't *need* them in order to love my home. In order for us CoMis to love our homes, we need a great mix of function, abundance, beauty, and simplicity. That's it. Just add love.

Do you want to love your home?
Stop decorating like someone else.

## What's important now?

—GREG MCKEOWN

# CHAPTER 4

# WHERE AND HOW TO START

Give Yourself the Gift of Focus

Knowing where to start is the first big step when it comes to creating a space that serves your family and represents your unique style. Focus bosses us in all the right ways and frees us from worrying about things that don't matter. I know you are itching to get started; you might even have some paint chips taped to the wall. We're gonna get there, but first we need to work out a few things.

It was moving day at the fixer-upper, and I immediately did what every respectable mother does. I set up all the beds and unpacked all the bathroom supplies. Sheets, cozy blankets, toilet paper, and toothbrushes—those were the necessities; everything else was secondary. It was hard and exhausting work, but I had a clear goal, and the threat of going toilet-paper-less was looming if I didn't meet it. With an air of authority, I successfully bossed my husband, Chad, into putting the beds together, and then I scurried around putting sheets on all the mattresses. My goal: the boys' beds had to be assembled and ready for occupancy by the time they came home from their new school so they could feel like they each had their own place in our new, unfamiliar home.

This was my mission, and failure wasn't an option. My boys needed this. When we have clarity and purpose, we find motivation and confidence. If you've ever been unsettled at home for any reason, I don't have to tell you that having one sane space in the midst of the chaos can make all the difference.

When home feels out of control, no matter what the reason, unsettledness and anxiety can seep in, and then the chaos becomes internal as well as external. Our home influences us both positively and negatively. It's wise to take notice and make a few small, immediate changes.

No matter what's going on in our homes, we all need at least one sane space. This applies especially to stressful times such as moves, transitions, and fixer-upper living. Every time my family moves or otherwise lives in the midst of chaos, the first thing I do is create *one* comfy, visually unmessy space. If you find yourself living in chaos, do not wait for the chaos to go away. If you do, you will be miserable for longer than necessary, which is the worst.

After that first phase of setting up all the beds and giving us each a private little island of calm in the sea of chaos, I started working on phase two, which was establishing a sane place where we could all be together.

At this point, we had already gutted the kitchen and were planning to eventually remove a wall near the family room. That mattered not. I painted the dark, hunter green walls of the family room bright white. Yep, I painted the very wall I knew was going to be knocked down. It took only a few hours, was a great excuse to do a crappy paint job, and effectively created a homey atmosphere. I put out a few throw pillows, even though I knew we'd have to repack them and cover everything up in a few months when we put up the drywall. Still, even Chad knew better than to question what was happening.

So in the midst of the chaos, we each had a little island of calm in our bedrooms and a larger island where we could be together without being forced to stare constantly at the mess and the undone. We needed a little win and a little progress. We needed one quiet space to give us a warm welcome at the end of a long day. Achieving this was worth the effort.

What I've just described is actually step two in a six-step process to prep your home to be cozy-minimalized. So far, you should have already completed step one from the last chapter:

> When we have clarity and purpose,
> we find motivation and confidence.

STEP 1: GATHER INSPIRATION by paying attention and pinning with passion.

STEP 2: CREATE ONE SANE SPACE. I know this is exciting and you are eager to start, but before you do anything else, I want you to create one sane space. If your home feels chaotic and overwhelming, you need to take back one room before you make any other changes. Start with one wall or one little corner you can retreat to during the chaos of making bigger changes in another space.

Maybe you've lived in your home for a while, but it's never felt finished and something just feels off.

Maybe your home is in transition, with drywall dust and a toilet in the yard.

Maybe you've had a recent move, and you are in the process of settling in and settling down.

No matter your situation, I want you to protect one space that can be untouched while other parts of the house are in transition. Or, if you're just moving in, take a day to create a zone of sanity where you and your family can relax together. This is self-care of the home, which means it is self-care of you and your family.

It's like when you decide to finally buy that ThunderShirt for the dog—you know, that tight dog shirt they sell on TV? The Fourth of July is coming up and there have been loud summer thunderstorms, and your dog is a bundle of nerves. So you get him a ThunderShirt to keep him from freaking out during thunderstorms and fireworks.

If you're going to create temporary chaos in your home, you need something like a ThunderShirt too. Why freak out if you don't have to? Make it a priority to create one sane space in the midst of whatever chaos your home is in right now. And it's okay to change the location of your sane space, depending on which room is in progress. Just make sure you always have someplace that's protected.

We can't put off living in our homes until that blissful day when things are finally perfect. Your family deserves to have a comfy place today, with pillows to nest in while watching *Napoleon Dynamite*, or an orderly place to have a meal together even if you don't have a kitchen—especially if you don't have a kitchen.

When things are weird and unpredictable, gift yourself and your people with a small space where you can relax and feel normal and not have to stare at the undone.

*We can't put off living in our homes until that blissful day when things are finally perfect.*

See, the second step is easy. Two easy steps so far—gather inspiration, and create one sane space. Decorating isn't so hard!

STEP 3: PICK ONE ROOM. Listen, I know you want to redo every room starting right now or else you might just burn it all down. Maybe you are so motivated and ready to get it done, you are committed to going without sleep until it's finished. I love that about you.

Or it could also be that you are beginning to wonder if this book is for you because you don't consider yourself creative or you don't "decorate." Do you think I wrote this book for people who already know how to do this? No, I wrote it for you. So let's break it down for clarity. Styling or decorating a home is simply making some logical decisions about how you use your home and how things in your home work together. You get to decide how you want to use each space in your home. You're already good at that! See, half the battle is simply paying attention to what you need to do in every room. Next you get to make decisions based on that. Each decision involves a little logic, your personal preferences, and universal decorating truths working together to help you create what you love. *We can do this!*

But we aren't going to change your entire house in two days. No. Instead, we're going to take it one room at a time.

If you've ever been in debt and then had to learn how to get out of debt, you know about the debt payoff snowball. If you owe money on five different credit cards, you pick the one with the lowest balance and focus on paying it off first. Some people say that's bad advice and you should first pay off the card with the highest interest rate. Logically, that makes sense, but emotionally, we are motivated by little wins. So paying off that first low-balance card gives us the motivation and positive momentum to tackle the next credit card. That's the debt payoff snowball.

A similar principle applies to decorating a home. If you are really overwhelmed, consider starting with the room that's closest to feeling done.

Don't choose the room with the biggest issues. You need a little win, a little snowball action.

If you are just moving in, start with the basics. The urgency of setting up house after you move lasts for a few weeks while you organize the pots and pans (unless you are renovating your kitchen), locate the lightbulbs for the lamps, and unpack the boxes. It's obvious what needs to be done, and there are annoying visual consequences to not doing it. Do those things first.

But once the basics are tended to and you set your sights on cozy-minimalizing your space, it won't be long before overwhelm will set in. You finally have your own place or you're finally ready to be intentional with the place you've had for a while, and suddenly every idea is an option. What should you do first? Wallpaper, paint the ceilings, take down walls, paint the window trim, change the fireplace, redo the kitchen, refinish the floors, update the bathroom, landscape the yard? You can make a convincing argument for starting with all of them. Then you'll question why you ever thought this was a good idea and start looking online at new houses for sale. When everything is an option, it can make you want to take a big nap in your curtainless, rugless bedroom with the lighthouse wallpaper border.

It's time to eliminate some options. You are going to limit the decisions you feel you need to make right now by choosing where to start—and once you have a starting point, you aren't going to worry about any other rooms. I want you to start with a room that has actual furniture or will need actual furniture. Save the kitchen, hallway, and bathroom for later—those will be easy once you get the method down.

You might want to start with the most annoying room. Or the most public room. Or your bedroom. You've already gathered inspiration for every room, and maybe you're feeling especially inspired over a certain space—choose that one. There's really no wrong room, and this method applies to every room of the house. Remember, though, to try to set yourself up for a win—don't pick the most complicated room as your starting point.

Got your one space picked out? Great! We are going to work through this room together for the rest of the book. Then you can apply the Cozy Minimalist method to every room of your house. It will end up being second nature, and you won't really even have to think about it after a few rooms. You are doing this! And I know you—you want to skip ahead, right? But don't you dare try to do this out of order. That's one of the most important parts of this entire process—don't get ahead of yourself.

STEP 4: WARN THE FAMILY. Let the other people who live in your home know what you are doing so they won't be caught off guard. Pets will just have to deal.

STEP 5: CONSIDER THE PURPOSE OF YOUR SPACE. My sister-in-law, Sheri, and her family live in a three-bedroom house with a family room, dining room, and eat-in kitchen. Their two teenagers are into music and crafting, and as their talents and interests have grown, their bedrooms have begun to fill. Then they were given a real piano, but there was no place to put it. They had a space problem. But when Sheri considered the purpose of every room in her house, she realized that they used the dining room only a few times a year.

Here she was, trying to make great use of every inch of her home, but because the builder called one room a dining room, it was bossing her into assuming she needed to use it as a dining room. Until she didn't. When she evaluated how they truly used their space, she decided she could reclaim an entire room. She sold their dining room furniture and instantly gained an extra room in her home that now holds a real piano and crafting supplies fit for a young Martha Stewart.

Every room needs a purpose, and this is the time to decide how your room will best serve you and your family for the next few years.

If you want a big change, you'll have to change big things. You don't go to the hairdresser and say, "I want a big change, but I don't want to cut or color my hair or do anything drastic." She will roll her eyes at you. Same with your house. If you hate everything and want a big change, then you'll need to make some big changes. This is gonna be fun!

In this step, you get to imagine your future in the room you are working on. Even if you've been living in your house for years, this is not the time to think about how you've used this room in the past. You are planning for the next few years and how you hope to use this room.

How might your family need to use this space in the next three to five years? Get out a little notebook, or get all fancy with a clipboard, and make a list of the ways you hope to use this room. Here are some questions to prompt your thinking.

- What activities will take place in the space?
- How many people do you need to seat comfortably?
- Do you need privacy or to block out the sun?
- Will people eat here?
- What kind of storage is needed?

Answering these questions will help determine the seating, surfaces, storage, privacy, coziness factor, lighting, flooring, and other materials you'll want to incorporate.

One of the things I love about our home is that it has a real wood-burning fireplace. It was one of the top five great things about this home that I focused

on when we purchased it. But after living here for a few years with our three big teenage boys and using our family room to the fullest extent—meaning binge-watching *The Office* and *Lost*—and with comfort high on my priority list, our fireplace has been practically forgotten.

When I considered the people I needed to serve here (our entire family of five), how I wanted to serve them (with comfort, so they would stay a long time rather than holing up alone in their bedrooms), what we wanted to do together (watch crappy TV), and the resources we had (no money for buying new sofas or redoing the fireplace so we could hang the TV over it), I realized I had to come up with a temporary (three-year) solution that looked good enough for me not to be embarrassed and served our family.

All of that is to say, anticipate any problems you might need to solve in regard to this room.

STEP 6: IDENTIFY SOLUTIONS, even imperfect ones. I decided to put a low settee smack-dab in front of the fireplace so our entire family could watch a show together. Not only did I put a glorified love seat directly in front of the biggest and most prized focal point of our entire house, I took the back legs off the settee (small miracle: the hearth is the exact same height as the legs—this was meant to be!) and set the piece right on the hearth itself. It is *so* undeniably honky-tonk to remove the back legs and set the settee on the hearth, but y'all, it gave us a much-needed nine inches of additional space! This is not Martha-approved—heck, it's not even something I want to admit in public—but it works, it helped our family, and I was okay with it because I knew it was temporary.

In my perfect world, I'd have a comfy chair on either side of the fireplace. A pair of chairs would look so much better than a settee with only two legs. The problem is that only one of the chairs would have a view of the TV, and then we wouldn't have enough space in our small family room for all five of us to watch TV together. As much as it's politically incorrect to admit it, our family *likes* to watch TV together. I tried several different seating arrangements in this room, but when I brought in the settee, Gavin, our youngest, begged for it to stay. So that's his headquarters—I even brought in a big coffee table so he could do his homework there.

You will never find me complaining about my teenage boys hanging out in our family room in the middle of everything. Sometimes I wonder if most of us have gotten things backward when it comes to kids and their stuff. When they are little, we think we have to allow their toys to take over all the public rooms of the house, but when they become teenagers, we banish all of their stuff to their rooms. Our family has done the opposite. When our boys were younger, we allowed one basket of toys permanent residence in the family room and put some kid-size wooden chairs around the coffee table—that was it. The family room wasn't a holding spot for all the toys. We'd occasionally build a temporary train track or a pillow fort, but for the most part, toys stayed in the boys' bedrooms or in a dedicated playroom. Now that the boys are older, I still want them to hang out in the family room as much as possible, but without it becoming their dedicated space. I encourage hanging out by providing good seating with everyone in mind, surfaces for homework, and a place for them to store stuff like homework supplies and charging cords. All right there in our family room.

I'm okay with this for a few reasons, but mostly because I know it's temporary. My youngest man-boy is in high school, which means he's going to get to watch crappy TV shows with us for only three more years. Our oldest is going to college this fall, so there won't be as many of us hanging out together on a nightly basis. This is why it's important to constantly reevaluate how a room can best serve your family. Families change quickly, and you don't want to wait around for perfection to enjoy your home together. We have big plans to remodel the basement into a comfy family room with space enough for everyone to laugh at Michael Scott or Leslie Knope without blocking our fireplace. Until then, we are using what we have in a way that serves us the best and still looks good enough that I like being home.

It's all about trade-offs. I'm willing to allow the family room to serve us well even though it's not my favorite look, because it is a look I can put up with. I also know that one day, we'll all be hanging out in the basement anyway, and I can take back my fireplace.

If you fall into the trap of waiting until you have a perfect solution to every design dilemma before you decide to make a room better, you might live with an untouched room for years. This is a sad waste, and I don't want you to do this any longer. A Cozy Minimalist embraces imperfect solutions. Yes, you'll still have an imperfect room, but in the meantime, you'll have a room that looks pretty great and serves your family.

I know how intimidating it can be to take action in a room when you know you can't perfect it. You get scared that you'll be stuck in your temporary fix and never finish your space because you'll forget about your goal. Don't worry; I have a plan for that, and it starts in the next chapter.

But before you move on, I want you to finish the steps in this first phase. Gather your inspiration, create your sane space, pick a room to work on, warn the family, consider the purpose of your space, and identify solutions you need to implement. From here on out, we'll work on one room together.

Throughout the rest of the book, I'm going to work through my own family room redo, so I can share photos of what the process looks like in real life. You'll work on your room while I show you what it looked like as I worked on mine. This is why you haven't seen many photos of our family room so far; I've been saving them.

Of course, I'm writing this book a few years after I first applied the CoMi steps to my house, so I'm recreating the kinds of issues I've dealt with in my various homes through the years, along with the decorating traps I used to get caught up in. You'll see *before* photos that represent how I used to approach my home as a Stuff Manager. And in each chapter, I'll share photos that show what it looks like to apply each step.

And friend, please know that there wasn't anything *wrong* with my stuff. We should all surround ourselves with pretty things, and I was doing that. The problem was that even when I was surrounded by stuff I liked, I still didn't like my room, it wasn't serving us in ways we needed, and as much as I hated to admit it, the room was overwhelming me.

As Cozy Minimalists, we want to get the most style out of the least amount of stuff. When we know our goal, it makes the decisions easy.

Unnecessary noise is the most cruel absence of care that can be inflicted on the sick or the well.

—FLORENCE NIGHTINGALE

# CHAPTER 5

# QUIET

Let Your Space Speak

These photos are recreations of our family room before I followed the Cozy Minimalist steps. As a Stuff Manager, I continued to add more stuff into my home without much thought. Even though I liked each item, together they created a room that felt all wrong. Instead of having more style with less stuff, our home had more stuff, but less style. You'll see the progression of this room throughout the rest of the book.

Let's recap where we are in this process.

First, either you've decided that you are a Cozy Minimalist, or you're at least interested enough not to throw this book away. You are fed up with all your stuff as well as with the indecision, overwhelm, and distraction your house is causing you.

You've gathered inspiration by pinning (or some equivalent) with passion and conducted a Pinterest reading to help you identify your style.

You've successfully ThunderShirted and created your one sane space, and this protected area of normalcy is ready to go.

You've picked out the room you are going to concentrate on first.

You've identified your room's purpose—right now and in the near future.

You've accepted that some solutions may be imperfect, at least for a time, and you're okay with that—perfection is not the goal.

You have done so much already. Most people never put this much thought into their home. Now it's time to make some actual changes in your chosen room.

When you've been living in a space for a while, it can be hard to see the possibilities.

ABOVE Before Cozy Minimalism, I tried to use lots of small items to bring style to this room. Nothing had much presence, and there's no focal point of the room other than the black firebox.

Quieting your space is a simple practice that will jump-start your creativity and give you a fresh perspective. It's kind of like a body cleanse for your home, only there's less time spent in the bathroom (unless that's the room you're decorating).

If an empty room is visually quiet, a full room is visually loud. A room slowly gets louder as we add furniture, accessories, and everyday items. Each item in your room has a voice and adds to the chorus of the room. The more stuff you put in a room, the louder it gets. We often don't even notice the visual roar our rooms create until we make them quiet. It's time to quiet your space. You are going to remove as many voices as possible from your room so you can see it with fresh eyes. This means you're going to temporarily take a bunch of stuff out of your room and give it a chance to breathe.

Quieting a space is something I've done for years, and this practice always has a profound effect on my ability to identify what I need in a space. I'm always

> Quieting your space is a simple practice that will jump-start your creativity and give you a fresh perspective.

a little surprised how quieting a room motivates and teaches me. It allows me to see my room a little differently and uncovers things I've been trying to hide from myself, such as walls that need paint, stains that need attention, and furniture that needs to be replaced. I'm really good at hiding things from myself, and I bet you are too.

## HOW TO QUIET A ROOM

This is going to be *such* fun, but also a little uncomfortable. I really believe that rooms can tell us some of what they need if we take the time to listen. So this is where we are going to start. You are going to remove everything from the room except the largest pieces. If you are working in your family room, you'll remove all the pillows, lamps, plants, books, wall art, clocks, photos, magazines—everything. You'll even want to remove the drapes. Yep. They probably need to be cleaned anyway. To do this right, you'll even roll up the rug. You better believe it. And you'll want to empty those bookshelves. The degree to which you whine and complain about this part is likely an indicator of how long it's been since you've done any of these things. The more you grumble and start to wonder if I'm playing an evil trick, the more likely it is that there is excess stuff you probably aren't appreciating or using. The harder this is, the more important it is that you follow through, and the bigger the payoff.

Remember, if you want big change, you have to make big changes. The more stuff you can get out of the room, the better off you'll be.

Now you are wondering where in the world you are going to put all of this stuff, right? Figuring that out is actually part of the assignment. And the pain-in-the-neck work is a reality check about how much you actually have. If you have so much in a room that the thought of moving it all out makes you want to die, that's a red flag. That doesn't make this method bad or wrong; it simply means you have a whole lot of stuff. Which, again, just proves how much you need to do this.

The good news is you aren't going to get rid of anything just yet (unless you absolutely know you don't want or need it). See how risk-free this is?

ABOVE Our fireplace, quieted. I was ready for a change in furniture for this room, so I even moved the chair and dresser out to see if I could come up with a better solution. Not shown in this photo are the sectional sofa and the TV and TV stand—that's all that was left in this room when quieted.

# If you want big change,
## you have to make big changes.

I'm not going to tell you to make all sorts of editing decisions now. You are simply going to get reacquainted with your space and let the room tell you what it needs and doesn't need. That way, you can make decisions with confidence.

You'll need to find a temporary holding place for everything from this one room. Yes, another part of your house will look cluttered for a few days or a few weeks. That's fine. This is how people do projects. It will get messy before it gets better—that's a sign of progress, so give yourself a high five.

Find a place to stash your stuff. I've put things outside on a porch and covered them with a tarp, stuffed artwork under my bed, placed everything in the basement. I don't care if you have to put things in the trunk of your car; you *must* find a place out of the room you are working on to relocate all the stuff that's been filling it up—ideally, a place that doesn't make your husband want to divorce you. This is where warning everyone ahead of time pays off. You don't want to unnecessarily annoy your family while you are doing this. In fact, after you spend a day with your quiet space, feel free to move a lamp and a pillow back in if they are routinely used and needed in the room. We want to keep everyone as happy as possible during this process.

Relocating everything will obviously be messy and weird, but the end result will be worth it. Yes, this is inconvenient. Yes, this is work. Anything worthwhile is both. You'll know you did it right if the only things left in your family room are a sofa, a chair or two, a coffee table, the TV, and whatever the TV sits on.

Plan to quiet your space during a time when you'll be able to spend some quality time, preferably during the day, with your room. Don't quiet the room the day before you leave for a three-week vacation on the French Riviera.

You might have an introverted room, and it could take a bit of time for your room to speak up. That's why it's important to keep the room hushed for at least a few days. In a perfect world, you'd give it a week.

When you quiet a space, something magical happens. Your room has a chance to speak to you. If every item—no matter how big or small—has a little

ABOVE Here are all the little decorative items I removed from the room. Don't worry, you don't need to display yours. I did this only to show you how most everything lacked presence. Even though I like each item, most aren't large enough to have a visual impact in the space.

voice, a room can get so loud it becomes a rumble you get used to, block out, and then ignore. When you remove all but a very few of these voices, you can start to listen to your space again. Now you get to pay attention. Give your quieted space some time to settle and do its work. When you start to notice things, you know you are on the right path.

With the drapes down, you realize you never finished painting the walls.

With the rug gone, you remember how much you love the wood floor.

Without the bookshelves, you see how large the room truly is. And you wonder why you need all those shelves anyway.

When you take down the artwork, you feel happy—or afraid or sad.

These are all really useful things to be aware of because these insights are your room speaking to you. Pay attention to these thoughts and decide what needs to change.

## FIND THE SILVER LINING

Once all your extra paraphernalia is moved out and you've spent some time feeling all the feels in that hushed-up room, you will go through the five stages of decorating grief. This is normal, so be sure to start diffusing your essential oils or cue up a funny show on

Netflix and stock up on your favorite lactose-free ice cream in preparation for what you are about to go through. Here's how it's going to go down.

1. Denial. Surely this cannot be the same house I was excited about moving into years ago.
2. Anger. I'm suing the real estate agent who sold us this house (or the landlord who owns this house).
3. Bargaining. To husband: If we can get a new sofa, you can buy that motorcycle and adopt that Great Dane dog family you've been wanting.
4. Depression. I hate everything. This house is hopeless. Maybe I can get a tax write-off if I donate it to the fire station so they can use it for a controlled burn.
5. Acceptance. There is no way out, so I guess I just need to move forward and do the next thing. Maybe I can fall in love with this place again, or for the first time.

This is a good time to look back at all the inspiration you gathered. If possible, look back through all those photos you collected while pinning with passion, and do it *while you're sitting in the room you're working on*. Slowly, you'll turn the corner from seeing what the room lacks to being enamored with what the room has to offer. You'll get excited about the possibilities. When you find yourself in a place of gratitude and excitement for this room, you know you're doing it right. It doesn't mean you delude yourself into thinking everything is perfect, but you truly begin to believe this space has good things to offer. I believe that every room has a silver lining. Your job is to find it.

For people like us who don't want to get rid of decorative stuff because we might need it in the future, quieting the house is the first step to decluttering. Once you apply this sweet little method to every room in your house, you'll have the confidence to get rid of the stuff you no longer need. It's a great way to trick yourself into getting rid of stuff, because you're gonna love your space so much you won't want it junked up anymore! You are finally going to have a plan for this room, and the confidence to know what you can and can't use in it. If you can't use it, you'll let it go. You'll be *happy* to let it go!

> Too often, we don't take a step forward because the next step doesn't match up with our dream.

Another magical thing happens when you quiet a space, especially if you are living with another human. He or she will also start noticing things in the room that have been forgotten. Repairing that crack, changing out the carpet, and getting new blinds will suddenly seem like needs (especially if they really are) because you aren't covering all this stuff up with cute throws and drapes and averting the eye with a great family photo. So many good things happen when you decide to quiet a room—and you haven't even had to step into a furniture store!

## TEMPORARY FIXES

In a perfect world, we'd all hire Chip Gaines or Nate Berkus to renovate our homes to imperfect perfection. In the real world, we have to make choices and hope to have enough money to call up that handyman down the street who drives the kidnapper van when we need to fix the plumbing. There are always trade-offs in life, and choosing what to do when is one of them.

Right from the start, it's helpful to decide which things in your space can be changed now and which require temporary fixes. The settee with two legs sitting on the hearth in our family room is a temporary fix. I'm okay with it because I know that in a year or so, we'll be able to change it. Meanwhile, it serves our family and looks good enough. It's better than what was, but not as good as what can be. That's the beauty of a temporary fix.

Say you bought a house that has red carpet in the family room. You really want new wood flooring there, but it's connected to the dining room, which, naturally, is connected to the kitchen, and suddenly, new wood floors in the family room means new wood floors for the whole first floor. It's something you know you'll need to address eventually, but it isn't going to happen in the near future. Meanwhile, you have to live with red carpet. Or do you? Enter the temporary fix.

Temporary fixes not only offer a solution to a problem, they are an opportunity to take a risk and try something new because you know you are going to change it later. Hate the red carpet? Pull it up and paint the subfloor, then buy a huge area rug. You can always use it on your wood floors once you get them, move it to another room, sell it, or give it away. Temporary fixes serve you in your time of need with a semi-solution. You invest a little money and a little time in exchange for a good-enough change that makes your home a little more bearable, usable, and attractive.

Hate your sofa but aren't ready to buy the sofa you've had your eye on? Cover it with a chenille coverlet, sew slipcovers for it, neutralize it with fresh pillows, or replace it with a vintage sofa from Craigslist. These are all temporary fixes that can hold you over until you can get what you really want.

Too often, we don't take a step forward because the next step doesn't match up with our dream. So instead of creating a prettier room with a decent sofa, we live in a room we hate because we are holding out for the dream sofa. Don't do that.

## WHEN A TEMPORARY FIX HAS SERVED ITS PURPOSE

When we moved into our house, the floor on the enclosed back porch was dirty brown linoleum. On a whim, I painted it with gray porch paint. This was a great way to have a clean floor that looked better for a few years while we worked in other rooms of the house. Temporary fixing at its finest, right?

But there's an underbelly to the temporary fix. You could be a temporary fix abuser. Some of us are queens at performing them. Our entire life is made of them, and our drapes are held together with hot glue and a prayer.

Recently, I quieted the back porch and realized that the temporary fix had done its job. It was time for a permanent fix. The paint looked dirty and tired, and it was starting to peel. If I really needed to, I could have extended the temporary fix for another year with another coat of paint, but I knew the porch's time had come. This is the key: you have to know when the time has come to let go of temporary and embrace permanent.

We decided to tile the floor and finally get this room finished. But I'm so happy that for three years, I had a good-enough back porch floor, and now it looks even better. The temporary fix was 100 percent worth the trouble and allowed us to focus on other things while still making the room look a little better.

After you quiet your space, you will notice things that need attention, from paint to floors to lighting. For each item, decide whether it's something you need to live with for a while longer, if it's something that needs a temporary fix, or if it's something you can address permanently right now. This is the part where many folks end up deciding to do small repairs and updates and start feeling really good about themselves for finally taking care of that thing that's been nagging them.

A word of caution, however. If you feel you need to paint, and if it's been more than four years since the last time you painted, your wall color probably could use an update. But don't make any paint color choices now; wait until you work through chapter 8. Yes, I know it feels like the right time to paint because your room is emptier than it has been in a long time, but over the next few

ABOVE The settee in front of our fireplace was a temporary fix.

days and weeks, you might be making some decisions that could impact the paint color you will want. Trust me on this one; just wait to paint.

## FIND YOUR SEAN

If you own your home and no one in your family has much experience doing house repairs—tiling, hanging chandeliers, changing fixtures, knocking down walls, and such—it's definitely worth it to find your Sean.

When we moved out to our fixer-upper, we hired someone we had never used before to do the work in the kitchen. He had decent references. It was fine, and I'm happy with the work. But behind the scenes, the communication was kind of nonexistent. Once the first project was done, I knew we'd probably never use this fella again.

Then we found Sean.

We first hired Sean for a project because my parents praised the work he did in their home. Always ask around. This is the best way to find someone you trust to do good work in your house. Sean understood our vision, was a pleasure to work with, gave fair estimates, communicated well, and always did what he said he'd do. After Sean finished that first project for us, we knew we wanted his hands on every renovation project we tackled. I think of Sean as my house's doctor. Sometimes he comes over to check up on what we are doing; sometimes we just need advice; sometimes he does entire projects for us from start to finish. After four years, he knows our house better than we do.

When you hire someone to do work in your home, there are times they get in and out in a few hours. Depending on the project, they might be there day in and day out for weeks. They see you at your worst, they see your home at its worst, and you have to come and go while they are working. Ideally, you want someone you can trust with everything you have who also does great work. That's a Sean.

There are more Seans out there, and you usually have to deal with a few non-Seans before you find one, but it's worth it to keep looking. Once you find a Sean, treat him (or her!) right and he'll stick with you forever. When we lived in our last town, our Sean's name was Randy. Randy worked alone and a

little slower than others (remember, there are trade-offs), but the quality of his work and his trustworthiness made the slower pace more than worth it. If you know you are going to need work done in your house off and on in the future, make it a priority to find your own Sean. If you ask around enough, you'll find him, and if you're lucky, he'll also become a close friend.

## SPEND TIME IN YOUR QUIETED SPACE

Once you've spent some time with your quieted room and looked through all the inspiration you've gathered, you can move on to the next chapter. Make sure you get both quality time and quantity time in the space. Hang out in there while watching a show or reading a book (quality time), but also allow the room to stay empty for at least a few days, or even a week (quantity time). You'll know you're ready to move on when you have some fresh observations about your room, when you are excited about possible changes you can make, and when you are no longer panicked that your room is empty.

Accept, bless, give
thanks and get going.

—SARAH BAN BREATHNACH

# CHAPTER 6

# WE CAN
# ARRANGE THAT

## Furniture Comes First

ABOVE Time for a permanent fix. Three years after moving in, we finally hired Sean to get rid of the popcorn ceiling and create a paneled ceiling look.

BELOW I replaced the settee with two chairs that I've had forever. I always shop my own house before I try the furniture store.

You quieted your room! I'm so proud of you. Isn't it weird in all the right ways? You are already challenging yourself to experience thoughts and feelings in your home that most people try to avoid. You are training yourself to pay attention. You've taken some time to live with and listen to your quieted room; you've considered the temporary fixes and addressed them. Now it's time to find the best place for the big stuff that you left in your quieted room. It's gonna be fun!

## PLACEMENT

Every piece you own might not have a perfect spot in your house, but it does have a best spot. It's your job to find that spot based on what you have and how you need to use your rooms. The best spot for your favorite chair when you have a new baby might not be the best spot when you have a home office.

It's close to impossible to put words in a book that will tell you how best to arrange your space when I can't see your space, don't know what room you are working on, and have no idea what stuff you have.

But even if I were standing beside you in your room, I would do the exact same thing I do in my own house. I'd pour myself a tall glass of iced coffee, put on some banjo music, put my hair in a tight topknot, lock the dog outside, and start moving furniture around until the layout feels right. I've tried those little room planner grids, but they're never as accurate or simple as just moving the real stuff around. There is no shortcut for this. If there were, I promise you, I would have found it.

I want you to try your sofa on every possible wall *and* in the middle of the room. I want you to try it at an angle. I want you to consider trading it out for the sofa in the other room. Everything is up for grabs, and if you are going to do this right, you need to explore all the options so you can find the best layout for you and your family.

Your assignment for this chapter is to find the best placement for the furniture that will go into the room you've quieted. If you are getting a new sofa in two months, use your current sofa as a placeholder.

Here are four questions you can use to help you figure out where to place your sofa and other big pieces.

1. IS THERE A FOCAL WALL? Not every room has a built-in focal wall, but if yours does, you'll want to keep that in mind. For a family room, the focal wall could be a fireplace, a picture window with a view, a wall with the TV, or a combination of these. Ideally, you want to find the best place for your sofa in relation to the focal wall before you find the best place for anything else. The goal is to set up your room so that the majority of the seating is facing or angled toward the focal wall.

2. WHAT IS THE LARGEST PIECE? Push all your furniture out of the way except for your largest seating piece, which is most likely your sofa. The sofa is usually the biggest, most important piece in the room, so it gets priority. In the bedroom, the largest piece is usually the bed. Nine times out of ten, the bed feels like it's in the right place if it's on the wall opposite the door. But sometimes that's not possible, or sometimes you may want it to face a focal wall, just as a sofa would.

About the only time a sofa looks right when it's placed against the wall is when it's a corner sectional and it's in a corner. Always pull your sofa out from the wall at least a few inches. This lets the room breathe, creates white space, and makes the room feel bigger. Try it!

For now, don't worry about anything except the focal wall and the largest piece. Grab a friend and move that sofa around until it feels right. If you are working in a room with a TV, I give you permission to move that around as well. And I give you a pass if your TV is in a fixed spot (hardwired over the fireplace, for example) or moving it would require paying the cable guy to move the hookup. If your TV is mobile, then this first move is more fun because you get to find the best spot for both items at once.

I always give myself plenty of time with this. Yes, the rest of the house is in chaos (except for your one sane space, remember). Plus—eyes on the prize—you are doing this so you can finally make some decisions, get your home looking the way you've always wanted, and move on. Taking the time you need is so worth it!

Promise me you will try your sofa in every possible place in the room.

LEFT In the midst of the mess of new trim and scooting around furniture.

RIGHT I decided on a larger coffee table. Now to figure out which side tables work best.

Call the kids down to help scoot it around, slide socks or pieces of cardboard under the feet to protect your floors, and move that sofa everywhere it will fit to see how it feels. If you feel unsure, call a friend over (pro tip: this has to be a friend whose home you actually like) and ask her opinion. Your job is to find the best possible placement for your stuff in this room. It's okay if your sofa ends up back where it started. At least now you'll know for sure.

When it comes down to it, there is no right or wrong. You get to decide what is right.

Once you have your sofa in a place that feels right, bring in any other primary seating, find the best place for that, and then bring in any secondary seating.

3. WHAT IS YOUR PRIMARY AND SECONDARY SEATING? Primary seating is any object on which someone sets their tush every day. By that definition, a toilet is a primary seat—and it is. Primary seating is also your sofa,

ABOVE I tried that gold cube table everywhere, but in the end, it didn't make it in the room. Since the room was cleared out except for seating and surfaces, it was easy to test secondary tables like this in different areas.

your favorite chair, and the chairs at your dinner table. Primary seating deserves a little more attention, and we can feel fine about investing a little more money in it because it works harder than secondary seating. Be sure to find the best placement for your primary seating before you move on to placing your secondary seating.

Your largest piece and your primary seating might be the same thing. But that chair your husband sits in every single night is also primary seating, even though it isn't your largest piece. Most rooms have more than one primary seat unless you live alone and never have any other humans in your rooms.

Secondary seating is the extra seating you have around the house for guests. You don't sit in secondary seating every day, but you can't get rid of it because when your friends and family come, they need a place to sit. These are the chairs in the corners of the room or against the wall that you pull up to the dining room table when you have people over. Secondary seating doesn't have to be super comfy. You don't need anyone deciding they are going to stay forever because your chairs are so cushy; you just need those chairs to do their job by providing a seat. I like buying my secondary seating secondhand.

If you have a small house without many places to sit, do yourself a favor and opt for cushy seating at the kitchen or dining room table. We have a small house, and when our friends come over, the menfolk tend to end up in the comfy family room while the womenfolk end up spending the evening around the dining room table with glasses of wine. I am *so* happy I opted for the cushy dining chairs so we can all be comfy as we hang out. With all the men in the family room, the only available space for us is the dining room, which means I need all the seats at the table to be as comfy as possible.

I even try to have tertiary seating. Mostly because I like to say the word *tertiary*. If a gang of friends suddenly drops by, tertiary seating means they'll at least have a place to rest their heinies, even if it isn't ideal. Tertiary seating includes ottomans, poufs, and small tables that can double as stools. I even count some indoor-outdoor chairs on our porch as tertiary. If possible, I never want to be caught without enough places for people to sit. Tertiary seating quietly whispers, "We knew you were coming. We're glad you're here. We have a place for you."

If I'm having a particularly difficult time with furniture placement, I'll take some photos with my phone so I can see the room with fresh eyes. The truth is, the arrangement of your furniture doesn't make or break the way your room looks, but it does make or break the way you use and experience a room. You want it to look right, feel right, and work right.

The truth is, the arrangement of your furniture doesn't make or break the way your room looks, but it does make or break the way you use and experience a room.

For now, don't be concerned if there are weird gaps in your room. It just means we aren't done yet. Once your primary and secondary seating is in place, it's time to add surfaces.

## 4. WHAT SURFACES AND STORAGE DO YOU NEED IN THE ROOM?

I usually wait until after I place the secondary seating to bring in any surfaces and storage because, while seating can be tricky to place, it's relatively easy to swap surfaces with other things in my house.

By surfaces, I simply mean the things on which you set other things. These include coffee tables, side tables, bookshelves, and desks. Storage items like armoires, cabinets, trunks, and dressers can be surfaces too. Use only surfaces and storage that are truly needed to help the room serve its purpose.

Fight the urge to include items in a room just because they've always been there. One mistake I see time and again is the tendency to pack too much stuff in a room in the name of being organized. When I had a larger kitchen, I could easily store my slow cooker in a dedicated corner cabinet.

ABOVE Notice the surfaces: round table in the corner, the mantel, the white dresser in the opposite corner, and for now that gold cube is still clinging to hope that he'll make the cut. He won't.

Now that I have a small kitchen, I can't allow something I use three times a year to take up precious real estate. I keep the slow cooker in the basement. I used to think the goal was to put as much stuff as possible within reach. That makes life easier the few times a year when I need little-used things, but the rest of the year, it clutters my life.

Now my goal is to keep the things I use most of the time right at my fingertips. The stuff I rarely use but need to hold on to is kept in out-of-the-way places so that I can enjoy some uncluttered areas.

Depending on the room and how you use it, you might need to have appropriate surfaces and storage for your puzzles, lamps, laptops, drinks, and projects. Surfaces can also be used to help anchor your larger pieces. Anchoring is part of a relationship. If a piece of furniture is alone in the middle of the room, it can look like it's floating. You anchor it when you set another piece of furniture next to it, and that prevents it from appearing lonely.

Ideally, every seat in a room should have a surface close enough to set a drink on. Remember when you considered the purpose of the room and how you hope to use it? Well, if you want to be able to play games in your family room, then it's a priority for you to have the kind of surface that will accommodate game night. If you like to read in bed, you'll want a surface next to your bed that can hold a great reading light and a stack of books. Be sure your surfaces reflect your purposes.

## YOUR TV AND DIVINE PROPORTION

A Cozy Minimalist understands the reality of TV watching. We do it. We accept it. We want to make it as enjoyable as possible without the TV taking over our entire room. And the good news is, it *is* possible for your TV to look like it belongs and not like an evil villain in your otherwise lovely family room.

LEFT The TV looks balanced because it's sitting on a dresser that's wider and taller than the television. If the TV were any bigger, it would look strange sitting on this piece.

RIGHT Here the TV looks like it could fall off the stump. Even though the stump is larger than the TV, since it's tall instead of long, we still get that unbalanced look.

Everything in your room has a relationship to everything else around it. It's just like an outfit: a little family you created that all gets along together, from the shoes to the earrings, the shirt, the pants, and the belt. It doesn't all match; it just *goes* together and makes sense. That's what we want for our rooms.

The art on the wall has a relationship to what it's hanging above; the rug has a relationship to what sits on it; the drapes are related to the walls. Every item is positioned in a way that makes it look like it is getting along with the others, not like they are mad at each other.

When it comes to placing the TV, the biggest mistake we tend to make is using a surface that's the wrong size. We forget that just like everything else in the room, the TV has a relationship to the things around it—especially to whatever it sits on or hangs above. The key is to balance the two.

When it comes to finding the right balance for the TV, it's all about the divine proportion. Yep, that's an actual thing. The divine proportion or the golden ratio is a super mathy topic, and if you are bored, by all means, google it. (And if you really want your mind blown, look up the Fibonacci sequence.)

Basically, the divine proportion is a ratio that explains why things are pleasing to the eye when it comes to design. A simple principle to follow is the two-thirds rule. Say you have a dresser with a piece of art hanging over it. Those two items will look most balanced when the art hanging above the dresser is about two-thirds the size of the dresser. Mind-blowing, right? If you have a TV, the same principle applies—you just have to work backward.

The TV should be approximately two-thirds the size of the thing it's sitting on (or over) in order for it to look balanced. Trying to describe why this works is kind of like trying to explain why the color red is red. It just is. It looks balanced because it just looks balanced, but the divine proportion helps us understand why. You can study the divine proportion or just remember that two-thirds usually works. And I never measure; I just eyeball it.

## NOW, BACK TO THAT SOFA . . .

Since we're talking placement and largest pieces, it's time to talk about all our sofa feelings. I could write an entire book about sofas and our emotional well-being. I'll settle for half a chapter.

Guess what? I don't really care what kind of sofa you have. I promise never to judge you by your sofa or rug size or paint color, and if you have the right friends, they'll never care, either. Most of us just want to come over to your house and sit on a cleanish, somewhat comfy sofa and look at your face and listen and be heard. But we do want to come over. And that's where the sofa starts to matter.

I know that if you hate your sofa, either you'll not invite people over, or you'll invite us over, but you'll be so distracted by your hated sofa that you might as well be alone. You will not be able to connect with anyone when you are preoccupied with the state of your house. That's why I write books like this, even though I sometimes feel sheepish for writing half a chapter about how to choose a sofa because, in the grand scheme of things, it really doesn't matter. Except when it does.

Sofas are there to serve us. They are great for quiet conversation, movie watching, nap taking, and friend making. They are also one of the most expensive items most of us will ever put in our home. Sofa buying is not for the faint of heart. And the only thing worse than having a sofa you hate is having a sofa budget and being so overwhelmed by choices that you can't even make a decision.

I want to be the one to tell you how to buy a sofa because I simultaneously don't care what kind of sofa you have, and I know how important it is to you to like your next sofa. I'm the perfect person to help you with this decision because I've purchased sofas that I hated the moment they were delivered, and I've also bought sofas that I've loved, which means I've learned a few things along the way.

I bought my favorite sofa fifteen years ago. It's been slipcovered twice, and it's still going strong. I've had custom-made sofas (the fifteen-year-old one I just mentioned), and I have another sofa from Rooms to Go that has been fantastic for our family. You have to know when to pay more and when to pay less.

If you aren't yet ready to buy a sofa, don't read this part. I don't want you feeling bad about your sofa. And if you love your sofa, by all means, let it be and feel free to skip this sofa section.

## HOW TO FIND A SOFA YOU WON'T HATE TOMORROW

For years, I had no idea how to buy furniture. I loved a pretty house, I wanted to have people over, and I knew that a pretty house didn't really cost any more money than a house I hated—it just required making informed decisions. For the most part, sofas all cost about the same amount of money—sofas you love and sofas you hate are both cheap and expensive. You can stay within your budget and buy either one.

Here's something I've learned about sofas. Most sofas that have a distinct style stay current and help a room look great for the long haul. If a sofa has a definable and recognizable style, your chances of loving it longer go way up.

ABOVE My fifteen-year-old custom sofa, slipcovered.

ABOVE My ten-year-old Rooms to Go sofa still looking good. And yes, I do want to use those pillows on every sofa.

Not only do these sofas have a unique look, they usually have some fun history that explains how the style came to be.

Distinct sofa styles usually have distinct style names, such as:

- Chesterfield
- Tuxedo
- Camelback
- Traditional
- Mid-century modern
- Victorian
- Cabriole
- Lawson
- English roll arm
- Knoll
- Birch arm

A definable style equals presence. Presence is part of style and is one reason we curate the pieces that take up important space in the most important place in our life, our home. Remember, as Cozy Minimalists, we want to get the most out of everything we put in our home. Ideally, we want both form *and* function, meaning we want our sofa to be a style we love and also to be useful for our family. So when it comes to choosing a sofa, we gather up our confidence and choose one that will last *and* has a bit of style, because we need to like the way our home looks so that we can use it for a greater purpose. If an ugly sofa costs the same as a pretty one, let's choose the pretty one. Most likely, that will be the one that has stood the test of time. And guess what—those sofas almost always have a recognizable name.

Open any design magazine from almost any decade, and you'll see examples of almost every type of sofa style listed above in every issue. The next time you shop for a sofa, choose one with a distinct, recognizable style—a sofa with a name. This is the key to finding a sofa whose lines won't look dated in three years.

Styles of sofas rotate in popularity. A few years ago, Chesterfields were all the rage. But they really never go out of style. Today, you can still buy a Chesterfield sofa and work it into almost any design. It's a confident style, so it's timeless. It almost doesn't make sense—you would think that such a bold,

A definable style equals presence.

defined style wouldn't be timeless, but when it comes to sofa *styles*, it's not true. Fabric is a different story. The more neutral the color, the longer you will love your sofa. The more distinct the sofa style, the more presence and style it will bring to your home.

These distinctly named sofas are the cute shoes of the design world.

If your sofa is full of poofy pillow pockets and the style cannot be narrowed down to a name—besides *transitional*, *plush*, or *reclining*—it's probably going to be more difficult to work into a room that you want to love for the long haul. Transitional usually means the manufacturer can't think of anything else to call it. Plush is how it feels. And reclining is what it does.

Again, if you have a sofa like that and love it, then yay! You love your sofa. But if you have a sofa like that and can't figure out why you don't love it and why it isn't working in your room, this could be the reason why.

As a Cozy Minimalist, you want your sofa to have style so it serves more than one purpose. If your sofa is indescribable in all the wrong ways, your room might feel thrown together or sloppy. And if we are going for a simple, finished look, we want to take advantage of every piece. So the next time you buy a sofa, go for a distinct, named style that will stand the test of time (because it already has) and be something that speaks for itself, not something you want to hide behind designer pillows. If your sofa is oversized, indescribable, and shapeless, it might not add the right style to your space and therefore could cause hatred to grow in your heart one day in the future when you want to host a baby shower.

Overstuffed, undefinable sofas are the tourist sneakers of the design world. Listen, I have nothing against tourists who wear sneakers. I actually love those people because they are embracing their truth. Their truth is comfort above all else. They are confident in their tourist sneaker choice, they know they don't look the most stylish, and they don't care. Their purpose is not to look good; it's to be comfortable at any cost. You can still make an outfit look cute with some tourist sneakers, but you'll miss out on the wow factor you get with a finished look.

A Cozy Minimalist doesn't waste money on a sofa whose style fails to elevate the room, even if it is comfy. If you are reading this book, my guess is you want more than "comfort above all else." You need more. You need your sofa to be both comfy and pretty.

Our main sofa, the one everyone sits on the most, is in our family room. It's the first room you see when you come into our home, and that sofa is the only sofa in our house right now. This is where we sit together, where my boys nap when they are sick, and where the cats snuggle with my husband. Yes, I'm the bitter cat person because my cats love my dog-loving husband more than they love me. Anyway, this sofa has many uses.

Since this sofa is in the main room of the house, it needs to be pretty enough for me not to hate it. It also has to be comfy because it's the main sofa where we sit *every* night of our lives, and it must be nappable. Because I didn't want to replace it in two years, I decided to invest more money in it than I would in an average sofa. I needed something with a style and quality that would endure the test of time and heavy use. It was my job to find that elusive sofa, the one that fit our needs for that particular room.

But when we lived in a house with an extra room, and I needed a sofa bed that could be a durable sofa for the boys' playroom, I went to a big-box store and bought a denim-slipcovered sleeper sofa. We don't sit on it very much, but when we do, it's dogs and boys and markers. This sofa has a rip in it, which, like Katy Perry, ups its cool factor. Because we didn't have to sit on this sofa daily, I picked an inexpensive option, and it's still lasted a long time. We've had it for ten years, and it's still serving us well out in our barn-turned-gathering-space.

You'll need to decide what you expect of your sofa. A great sofa can last twenty years and one day be recovered and downgraded to another room in your house. Think about it. If you spend $950 on a sofa that lasts three years or $3,000 on a sofa that lasts fifteen years, which is the better deal?

If buying a sofa isn't an option, but your sofa is driving you mad, it's time for a temporary solution. My favorite temporary sofa fixes all involve covering the sofa. If you can sew, make a slipcover. If you like bright, happy colors, find a few quilts to throw over the sofa and anchor them with some large solid-colored pillows. My current favorite fix is to layer one or two neutral chenille bedspreads on a worn-out sofa. You get some fresh texture without drawing more attention to the sofa with lots of color and pattern.

Whether you are using a new or old sofa, an antique bed, or a handmade dining room table, the goal is to find the best possible placement for all of your furniture before you move on to the next step. Placing furniture in a room without art, rugs, or tchotchkes in the way allows you to truly find the best location for your pieces without forcing them to work with preexisting limitations. Without art on the walls, you won't be tempted to center the furniture under the art; instead, you'll get to decide the best place for the furniture based solely on where each piece works best in the room. Without a rug on the floor, you won't absentmindedly put the sofa where it's always been. When you add things into a space in the correct order, you'll end up with a room that feels intentional, serves your family, and looks great. Got your furniture in place? Well done. Now you are ready for the next step.

Order is the shape upon
which beauty depends.

—PEARL S. BUCK

CHAPTER 7

# THE
# DECORATING
# TRINITY

Rugs and Drapes and Lighting, Oh My!

ABOVE This rug is so small that it looks like the furniture is falling off of it. This is the wrong size rug.

If I had to shop for a room redesign before I saw it, here's what I'd bring: a *huge* jute rug, enough long drapes for all the windows, and three chunky lamps. If your seating and surfaces are comfortable and in the right place, and you add rugs, drapes, and lighting, then you are 75 percent of the way to a finished space. *Yes*. This is true.

By now, you've quieted your room and you are happy with the furniture arrangement. You've got seating and surfaces and storage all in the best places. I know you desperately want to toss some throw pillows on the sofa and hang some art on your walls, but I have one word for you first: *Stop.* There is an order for placing things in a room.

Getting the steps out of order is exactly what gets us into trouble. We see a blank wall and we immediately feel compelled to fill it. Not only that, the blank wall is so large that we decide the only way to conquer it is to make it a gallery wall—the highest level of decorating tedium and most difficult feat you will ever face when you are hanging wall art. Do *not* start with a gallery wall. If you do, you'll end up hanging things in places where they don't need to be and then wonder why they don't look right. You shouldn't put *anything* on your walls until your drapes are hung correctly. Why? Because drapes—as well as rugs and lighting—come before wall art—that's the order.

I repeat: *Do not hang anything on your walls until your drapes are hung correctly.* Go ahead and picture me encouraging you through a megaphone, chanting, "Don't start your art until your drapes are hung correctly!" More about this in chapter 8.

The order in which you place things in a room is absolutely crucial. When you incorporate larger, more impactful items like rugs, drapes, and lighting first, your room gets filled with style and coziness without using up much actual space. Think about it: even a large rug takes up almost no square footage in a room since it's flat on the floor, but it can add a huge amount of style and coziness. Placing a few large, impactful items first will save you from many late-night tears and early morning return lines. Following this method builds confidence, allows for less waste, keeps your space under control, and minimizes the risk of accidentally purchasing too many adorable yet useless accessories. Rugs, drapes, and lighting—in that order—are truly the cozifiers of every room and something all CoMis must take advantage of.

When your room feels wrong, the probability is high that the reason is one (or all) of these three issues:

1. The rug is too small.
2. The drapes are too short.
3. The lamps don't exist.

This is why we want all of our accessories out of the way while we are making these decisions—it's so easy to get distracted by a cute pillow, but first, we need to find the right size rug. Hear me out. I know what you are thinking: *But I already* have *a rug. Can't I move on?* No. Especially if your rug is 4 x 6 feet, floats under the coffee table, and dares anything else to sit on it.

A Cozy Minimalist makes decisions that focus on incorporating simplicity, coziness, function, and beauty.

Remember, decorating is about making decisions. A Cozy Minimalist makes decisions that focus on incorporating function, abundance, beauty, and simplicity. If those things are our goals, then most of the time a rug, drapes, and lighting are going to be the fastest, easiest way to get there without adding in a bunch of extra stuff. Each of these items on its own contributes a ton of coziness, beauty, and function. Rugs, drapes, and lighting are a CoMi's BFFs.

## RUGS

A large rug pulls a room together. It sets the style, color, and mood for the space and makes it feel high-end and finished. Yep, you can use a rug even on carpet. Small rugs (the kind where the rug is in the center of the room with only a coffee table on it and the sofa isn't even touching the rug) can make a room look more disjointed than a room with no rug at all. It's better to have no rug than to have one that's too small. But it's best to have a big rug.

If you've never experienced the effect the right size rug can have in a space, get ready to be amazed. I've been using big rugs in my house for fifteen years, and the moment a large rug goes down in a room, it still takes my breath away. It's decorating magic, and you have to experience it to feel its worth.

Almost every bedroom and family room can benefit from a rug. If you've never tried one, I want you to. If you have a tiny rug, it will only add more clutter. Rugs act as an anchor. Remember, we want all the things in our space to feel friendly toward each other. The rug connects all your large furniture.

Your goal is to have at least the front legs of your primary seating on the rug. This is why we place the furniture in the room before we choose a rug, so we know what size rug we need. In a family room, that means at least the front legs of the sofa sit on the rug. In a bedroom, you want to be able to get out of bed and comfortably walk around it with your feet on the rug. Rarely does a 5 x 8-foot rug qualify as a large rug. That's a big small rug. Five-by-eights work best in entryways and laundry rooms. Nine times out of ten, you'll need a much larger rug.

Rugs serve us well and earn their keep. They instantly add style to a room and cozy it up, making the space more comfortable for humans. That makes it a triple win, which is why large rugs are a CoMi's BFF.

LEFT This ten-by-fourteen-foot rug covers all but a two foot perimeter around our small family room.

RIGHT I layered a cowhide rug over in front of the dresser to extend and connect the floor space.

Don't worry, you don't have to go broke buying a rug. I love affordable natural jute rugs (unless there are babies or toddlers in the house—they are too itchy for little people to sit and crawl on). Wool rugs last forever, and if you buy one and tire of the style after a few years but keep it nice, you can usually sell it. I also love vintage rugs. Anything vintage that still looks good tells me that I can't ruin it. Think about it: if you buy a fifty-year-old Persian rug for $1,000 and it's been walked on for fifty years and still looks great, then you and your family probably cannot ruin this rug. This is when I do the math to convince myself that I'm not wasting my hard-earned money. Would you rather spend $400 for a rug that will last you three years, or $1,000 for a rug you'll keep for twenty years or more? I'm slowly adding antique wool rugs to my collection because I've learned I don't have to baby them. In fact, just the opposite—they've proven they don't need to be babied.

Here's the Cozy Minimalist magic—when you have the right rug filling a room, you suddenly need a lot less stuff. Rugs serve people so much better than random accessories. Even though they take more effort to get right, they'll ultimately serve our homes so much more. It took me a long time to trust this universal truth. Promise me you'll try it? If you don't believe me, go to the closest store that sells large rugs. Pick out either a large, neutral-colored rug with a simple pattern, or a large jute rug. Make sure you can return the rug. Bring the rug home and try it out. Bask in the magic.

I buy my rugs almost exclusively online, mostly because I've learned not to worry about getting an exact color match. Plus, I've learned that it's easier to paint a room to go with the furniture and rugs I have than to paint a room and then try to find rugs and furniture to match. It's also easier to find drapes to go with a rug than to find a rug that works with drapes. See why the order is so important? When I shop online for a rug, I usually stick with neutral colors. I read the customer reviews and buy from places that will let me return a purchase if I need to. If you've never purchased a large rug before, though, start local. That way, you can see, feel, and visit your ideal rug a few times before you commit. Over time, you'll gain more confidence in rug buying.

Using a large rug will change the way you decorate a room. I promise I

When you have
the right rug filling
a room, you suddenly
need a lot less stuff.

would never tell you to purchase something you don't need. If you want a cozy, finished, pulled-together home using the least amount of stuff possible, rugs are your secret weapon.

Once you have your rug, move on to the next step: drapes.

## DRAPES

If your rug is Oprah, your drapes are Gayle. Like rugs, they are a no-brainer addition to any Cozy Minimalist space. We get another triple win from drapes:

1. They cozy up a room because of their softness.
2. They can have actual function, such as closing for privacy or blacking out light for sleeping.
3. They add style and color to our space.

Let's let our drapes work for us in all the best ways.

Drapes hung high and wide expand a room visually. Drapes are one of the few things you can add to a room that actually make it look bigger. We Cozy Minimalists *love* drapes! The only problem is many of us are using drapes all wrong.

TOP Undraped windows.

MIDDLE Windows with 84 inch drapes that block too much natural light and, when hung above the window trim, don't even go to the floor (capris).

BOTTOM Ahh, drapes hung high and wide visually expand the space.

There are lots of different styles of drapes, but I'm going to classify drapes into two categories: decorative drapes and privacy drapes. Most of us purchase decorative drapes—what we can get off the rack at Target or West Elm. These are usually intended to decorate a window, not to be closed for privacy. Custom drapes or blackout drapes that are lined and weighted are intended to be opened and closed.

What difference does it make?

Have you ever driven by a house at night in which the unlined red drapes are closed, all the lights in the house are on, and the windows are glowing red? If so, you know it kind of looks like Satan is having a big, hot party. This is because someone is trying to make their decorative drapes do the job of privacy drapes. It looks really weird from the outside, and inside, it doesn't feel all that private.

If you want decorative drapes but you also need privacy, there are lots of options, such as adding blinds, shades, or interior shutters. This looks extra nice on the inside because you are getting more layers and style in your space without adding a bunch of junk to your surfaces. See how a Cozy Minimalist can really get on board with great window treatments?

Decorative drapes aren't actually made to be closed over a window. What? Yep. Because they are usually unlined, their main job is to enhance the window, not to block out the light that comes through it.

A CoMi will want to hang her drapes in such a way that, when open, the drapes fall against the wall on either side of the window. The inner edge of the drapes will just cover the outer edge of the window pane to create the illusion that the window keeps going on either side behind the drapes. This makes your window appear larger, which adds more visual interest yet still maximizes the view and natural light. Most people get a curtain rod that is too short and doesn't expand very far beyond the edges of the window. We want our drapes to naturally live in front of the wall on either side of the window, which means we need to provide enough additional space at both ends of the rod to hold the entire drape comfortably. That could mean your rod extends twelve to eighteen inches from the edge of your window on both sides.

But don't hang your rod yet—there is yet another way drapes can serve us if we hang them right. They can make the room look taller. What if I told you that you could buy a pair of pants that make you look either six inches taller or six inches shorter? You can. This is why most of us shy away from capris—they cut us off at a weird place and make us look shorter and squatter. Most women would prefer to appear taller and, hence, thinner, which means capris are out of the question. So why are we putting capris on our windows?

We put capris on our windows when we hang the rod right above the top of the window and the drapes end inches from the floor. This happens anytime we use 84-inch drapes. Eighty-four-inch drapes and 5 x 8 rugs are in the same class. They are mostly hurting rather than helping our efforts. We want to raise that rod, get some 96-inch or 108-inch drapes, and hang them high and wide. Ideally, you want your drapes to just barely skim the floor, or if you like the look, they can touch or puddle on the floor. If you do that, you'll be amazed at how it expands your space visually.

Drapes that are hung high and go all the way to the floor work wonders on a room. Let them. Use them; take advantage of them. Almost every room can benefit from drapes. I get mine from IKEA. Less than $40 for a pair of drapes that transforms my room.

If you have baseboard heaters, you might be mourning the fact that you cannot have long drapes. Yes, drapes to the floor are ideal, but not required. This is a great opportunity to try another interesting treatment on your windows.

*Every limitation has a beautiful workaround.*

Instead of using drapes, beef up the trim work around your windows, and add some inexpensive matchstick blinds or consider plantation shutters. Every limitation has a beautiful workaround.

## LIGHTING

Every room needs light. And lots of rooms have it in the form of one builder-grade overhead light, often in the center of the room. Now, the builder isn't suggesting that this is all the lighting you'll ever need. He's just doing his job of providing one overhead light so he can pass inspection. We can do better. Lighting is an opportunity for style and creativity. And, just as with rugs and drapes, lighting can serve more than one purpose if we let it. Not only do we need to see what we are doing in our houses, we can add a lot of style to our space just by choosing the right light. Cozy Minimalists love this because we get to kill two birds with one lightbulb.

I like to classify lighting into four categories: natural lighting, overhead decorative lighting, task lighting, and accent lighting.

NATURAL LIGHTING is available only in the daytime, but I always want to maximize it. That means I avoid any window treatments that permanently block natural light from my windows. I can close my blinds if I need to, but if not, I'll usually have them wide open. Natural light is free and the best light there is.

Whenever we are moving into a new house, one of the main things I look for is how much natural light there is and how big the south-facing windows are. Those windows get light almost all day long, and it's a beautiful, sparkly light that makes me feel like a princess. This is why we don't hang drapes in front of all of the window panes—we don't want to unnecessarily block any natural light. Natural light is the queen, and the drapes shouldn't diminish her ability to shine.

ABOVE I'm pretty sure Francie feels like a princess basking in all that natural light.

OVERHEAD DECORATIVE LIGHTING is a great opportunity to add style to a room but often a lousy way to light it. Ideally, lighting will add both form and function to our space. I used to try to demand both 100 percent form and 100 percent function from all my overhead lighting. It needed to do it all! But I realized that limited me on the types of overhead lighting I could use in some of my rooms.

Take our dining room, for example. If we are dining at night, we don't need the room lit up enough to do surgery. I want cozy, flattering light that helps me avoid eating my napkin. In my bedroom, family room, and dining room, I look for lighting that adds a huge amount of style and also decent light—this is overhead decorative lighting. But I know that this overhead decorative lighting is not going to be the only light I use, so the pressure is off to fully light every corner of the room. When I'm making a decision on overhead

LEFT This beaded chandelier (decorative overhead light) doesn't put off the best lighting, but she makes up for it in style

RIGHT Accent lighting over a niche illuminates a pretty vignette and adds personality to the kitchen.

decorative lighting, I err on the side of choosing the light that has the style I want more than the one that gives off the best light, because its main purpose is decorative. Heavy on the decorative, easy on the light.

OVERHEAD TASK LIGHTING is what you need in a bathroom, kitchen, or stairwell so you can do things like put on makeup without poking yourself in the eye, chop vegetables without losing a finger, and carry laundry up and down stairs without tripping. This overhead light needs to work hard because it helps you not to hurt yourself while living in your house. That means when it comes to choosing overhead task lighting, the actual light it provides is the priority over the style it provides. If there is a stylish overhead light you are in love with, but it doesn't give off good light, you'll need to either add more task lighting or find a different light fixture. While it's important to like the style of everything you put in your house, the top priority for overhead task lighting is to provide fantastic light.

ACCENT LIGHTING (such as a lamp) lights up one area of a room and provides enough light to do certain tasks, such as reading a book. Lamps are not purely decorative; they also help us do things without getting a low-light headache. If you don't have lamps, you are missing out. Most of us try to force our overhead lighting to do the job of lamps, then we wonder why we squint all the time, have a constant headache, and look fifty years older every night. Or we buy one lamp and wonder why our house still feels dark. Most rooms where people sit and hang out can benefit from at least three lamps. Book reading, paperwork, homework, computer work, puzzles, and anything you are looking at closely are best done with a lamp. Aside from soft candlelight, diffused light from a lamp shade is the most flattering light you can have in a room. I wish I could carry a lamp around with me everywhere I go. Overhead lighting isn't meant to help us do detail work, nor does it make us look our best. I try to avoid it.

There are also specialized accent lamps we can use to highlight things. We might hang a picture light over a painting or install small, round puck lights above a display shelf. This kind of accent lighting is useful for spotlighting items of special interest in your home.

Before you run out and buy new lighting, though, be sure to read chapter 9.

## WHY THE STEPS ARE SO IMPORTANT

When we don't follow the steps in the right order, here's what can happen. We move into a house, put our sofa across from wherever the previous owners had the TV cable installed, and hang something on the wall over the sofa so that our house will feel homey.

Because the sofa is large and the biggest piece of art we have is only twenty-four inches wide, we decide to create an accidental gallery wall. We scatter some art on the wall and then wonder why we hate our space.

The right motive is there, and I commend it, but the order is all wrong. We are doing ourselves a huge disservice by hanging art before it's time. Remember my megaphone? You absolutely, unequivocally never want to hang art in a room until your furniture is in the exact best place, the rug is placed, the drapes are hung, and the lighting is in position.

Why?

Because furniture, lamps, and drapes create different wall boundaries that we need our art to fill, and rugs might dictate the colors you decide to use. When we hang art after the drapes are hung, we'll be working in the correct space. Remember, when hung correctly, drapes often cover a little

Making good design decisions is less about knowing the trends and more about knowing the order to add things we truly need and use in a home.

part of the wall, so when you hang your drapes first, you know exactly where your wall boundaries are, and you'll have less space to fill. Instead of panicking, trying to fill up your echoey, non-rug-covered, non-draped space with lots of extra art to make up for the emptiness you feel in your room, you'll have confidence that everything is in place and won't need to overcompensate with extra art and accessories. Yippee!

This is the part where I beg you once again not to add anything extra into your room until you get the rug, drapes, and lighting right. Give yourself time to get this right. Give yourself grace to get things wrong on your first try. I probably return 25 percent of what I purchase for my house. It's hard to know if something is going to work until you get it in the room and live with it for a few days. Keep those receipts.

Making good design decisions is less about knowing the trends and more about knowing the order to add things we truly need and use in a home. Isn't that a relief? When the rug, drapes, and lighting follow your well-placed seating and surfaces, your room will be 75 percent done. That's definitely a relief! This is what separates the wise Cozy Minimalist from the foolish Stuff Manager. I wish I had known this years ago.

If everything is important,
then nothing is.

—PATRICK LENCIONI

# CHAPTER 8

# WALLS

## AND

# WALL ART

Bringing a Room Together

Everything in your home is related, and you want it all to be on friendly terms. You want your beautiful things to tell a beautiful, meaningful, and cohesive family story in the most Cozy Minimalist way possible. You want your home to be simple and functional and pretty without overwhelming you with a bunch of stuff. Your walls can help you do that.

When it comes to your walls, there are three categories of things you can use to dress them: wall treatments, wall art, and wall sabbaths. CoMis take advantage of all three in every room of their homes.

But remember, don't start your art until your drapes are hung correctly!

## WALL TREATMENTS

Wall treatments are permanent materials applied directly to the walls themselves. They include paint, wallpaper, murals, shiplap, paneling, tile, and many other surfacing products. Wall treatments are a great way to add interest to a room without bringing in a bunch of extra stuff. If you have a high need for coziness but don't want to burden yourself with ten million accessories or stacks of wall art, then wall treatments are the perfect option. Adding a

Adding a layer of texture or a bold color to the walls is an ideal way for a Cozy Minimalist to add style to a room.

layer of texture or a bold color to the walls is an ideal way for a Cozy Minimalist to add style to a room. I've seen rooms with practically nothing on the walls, but because of a well-chosen wall treatment, the room still felt cozy and inviting.

## TIME TO PAINT, WALLPAPER, SHIPLAP, AND MURAL

Once your drapes are hung, the rug is down, your lighting is in, and your furniture is all in place, the room will probably still need more presence, coziness, and style to feel right. This is when you decide whether you need to make a wall change. The most common wall treatment is paint, so I'll focus on that, but you can apply this same logic and time frame to whatever wall treatment you are considering.

Paint has magical powers to date a room (hello, burgundy and hunter green of 1992), and those same magical powers can freshen a room. If you haven't painted a room in five years, now is the time to consider a fresh coat. Paint is by far the least expensive way to make a huge change in a space.

Now that you have chosen your furnishings, surfaces, drapes, and lighting, it's the perfect time to paint your room. I know this probably seems counterintuitive. Why not paint back in chapter 5 when the room was empty and you quieted the house? Look around. It's so much easier to rehang a rod and hardware (just use the same holes; it's no big deal!) than to create an entire wall treatment only to realize once your drapes are hung or once you put the rug down that you didn't need to go to all that trouble in the first place. Or, worse, to realize that your paint color doesn't look right with your rug. Since there are so many paint colors to choose from, you want to get the rug and drapes right first, then pick a paint color that works with them instead of the other way around.

It should take only fifteen or twenty minutes to cover or move things out of your way to paint, so much less time than repainting an entire room because you chose the wrong color. Aren't you glad you waited? Otherwise, you might have had to repaint at this point, and that's a bigger pain than moving and covering a few pieces of furniture and dismounting the drapery rod.

## WALL ART (WHERE *NOT* TO START)

For the sake of our mutual sanity, I'm calling everything you hang on your walls "art." This term applies to the clipboard holding the watercolor your sister gave you, the big clock you bought at Target, the chippy shutters you found at the antique mall, the hand-lettered verse on a canvas, and that Monet you stole from the museum. If it's hanging on or leaning against your walls, in this book, we're calling it art.

When it comes to wall art, sometimes it's easier to start by knowing what *not* to do. I'm the queen of this because everything I'm going to tell you not to do, I've done. I've broken all the rules and had to figure out the hard way—with a wall full of nail holes—why something just wasn't working. It was worth every nail hole.

The two biggest mistakes to avoid are buying art that is too small, and hanging mirrors and reflective glass in the wrong place.

AVOID BUYING ART THAT IS TOO SMALL. One large piece of art is more substantial visually, which results in its naturally having more style—and it also results in feeling like we are taking a bigger risk. Because we are. Yes, it seems less risky to buy ten $15 inspirational quotes in 8 x 10 frames over the course of a year and then try to find places for them here and there. (I call this "scatter art.")

But what if you used that $150 and bought one large piece of art you loved that allowed you to make a big style statement? Large art can make the difference between a room that feels pulled together and a room that feels choppy. Statement pieces set the mood for your home, and large art can be your secret style weapon.

My favorite way to find large art is to go to an antique mall and shop for old, chippy shutters, fence gates, or large architectural pieces. Sometimes I'll find a big, ugly canvas painting at the thrift store and then paint an abstract design over it using leftover wall paint. It actually costs less than buying a new canvas from the craft store. Large mirrors are a CoMi's no-brainer option (we'll talk more about mirrors in a moment). They are beautiful, the frames can be painted any color, and they make a space look bigger because they reflect light. Plus, they are useful for adjusting your hair as you pass by. Large art sets the tone for a space in one fell swoop. Take advantage of that.

Look back at those Pinterest boards you created. Specifically, look at the wall art. What do you notice? My guess is size and risk. I bet you'll notice larger statement pieces in rooms you love. You'll see large focal pieces instead of

ABOVE An example of a wall treatment I used in our bedroom. I painted imperfect white dash marks over the dark wall to create some interest and whimsy and to fill up wall space.

lots of smalls. These pieces have presence, which adds style rather than distraction to a room.

Resist the urge to continually add scatter art. We gravitate to that not because it's meaningful or beautiful, but because we feel a need to fill empty space. It's not only okay but good to have some empty walls in a house; it puts more attention on those walls that are beautifully filled.

If you have an unusually large expanse of walls, you might need to imagine the room in zones. Break up larger areas into smaller zones and hang your art accordingly. It's easier to allow for white space—a wall sabbath—when you think of your room in zones. We'll talk more about wall sabbaths shortly.

AVOID HANGING MIRRORS AND REFLECTIVE GLASS IN THE WRONG PLACE. My mom always says never to buy a painting of a scene if you wouldn't want to be there. So if you have a choice between a painting of a stormy ocean and an English meadow, pick the one where you'd actually like to be.

LEFT As you walk into the bathroom, the mirror reflects interesting tile work and a fun shower curtain.

RIGHT Too much word art in a room is overwhelming. Aim for only one piece of readable art per space.

It's not only okay but good to have some empty
walls in a house; it puts more attention on
those walls that are beautifully filled.

Mirrors show a scene too. Perhaps the most important thing to remember about a mirror is that its artwork is what it reflects. If you hang a mirror and don't love what it reflects, it's like hanging a piece of art you don't like. Why would you do that? Oftentimes, we hang a mirror above a mantel and don't realize we could get the same look by hanging a large photo of our ceiling fan there instead. I can't imagine a situation in which you would buy a portrait of your ceiling fan, much less hang it over your mantel. Always consider what a mirror reflects in a room before you hang it. Hang mirrors so they reflect a part of your home that you like looking at. Also, try to avoid leaning a mirror on your mantel unless you like looking at the underbelly of your ceiling fan.

The same principle applies to any piece of artwork framed under reflective glass. Hung in the wrong place, the only thing you'll ever see when you look at that art is a reflection of the room. Basically, you just hung a mirror. Hang a glassed-in piece of art across from a window and you'll never actually get to enjoy what's behind the glass, only a reflection of what's outside the window. There are three ways to remedy this:

1. Find something not under glass to use in its place, and hang the art with glass in an area where there won't be a reflection.
2. Take the art to a frame store, and have the reflective glass switched out for non-reflective glass.
3. Remove the glass.

Be sure to have some artwork in your home that has no glass at all. When everything is framed behind glass, it can feel untouchable and overly store-bought. Consider adding in some textured art such as an oil painting on canvas, a piece of fiber art or tapestry, or some type of wood piece.

Now that we've covered mistakes to avoid, it's time to hang that art!

> Art wants to be friends with the other stuff in the room.

## WALL ART (WHERE TO START)

Sometimes you'll have a favorite piece of art that looks good on every wall. How do you know where to hang it? I like to prioritize my walls. Pretend you can put art on only one wall in your room. Which wall deserves or needs art the most? That's your priority. Sometimes that's the wall above the fireplace; sometimes it's the big, empty wall in the room. Sometimes it's the wall over the sofa. Find the priority wall. I won't even touch the other walls in a room until the priority wall is right. You don't want art on a non-priority wall to limit what you can do with the most important, priority wall. Once you get the right piece on your priority wall, figure out what wall is the next priority, and repeat the process.

Your goal as a Cozy Minimalist is to first figure out what size space you want to fill with your wall art. The good news? You already know how to do this! Remember the divine proportion back in chapter 6? You already have your furniture in place, right? So now, if you want art above it, you know the art should be about two-thirds the size of what it's hanging above in order to look and feel balanced.

Now look for something to fill that space!

Once you've identified your priority wall and have picked out some wall art, the next step is to think about your art in relation to the other things in the room. Art wants to be friends with the other stuff in the room.

ABOVE Because I placed the lamp in the room first, it limited how much wall space I had to work with. I was able to hang the cabinet in the correct spot, off-center, so I could open the door without hitting the lamp. If I had hung the cabinet first (art before the lamp), I probably would have centered it. There wouldn't have been room for the large scale lamp, and the cabinet would have felt too small to hang over the dresser. Working in order solves all sorts of potential problems.

Think of the items in your room like the pieces of an outfit—you don't need them all to match perfectly; you just want them to make sense together.

Begin by leaning your art against the wall to make sure it feels right in the space. Let it live there for a few hours, and see how it feels when you walk into a room. Then try hanging pieces closer to furniture than you might be used to. So many times, I'll see a beautiful sofa, but the art is hung so far above it that I wonder if the sofa has some contagious disease the artwork doesn't want to catch. Art should relate harmoniously to the things around it, just like everything in your home has a relationship with what surrounds it. This is a great time to look back at your inspiration photos to see where the art is hung in relation to the furniture in a room.

Some people will give measurements, like hang your art so that the center of it is sixty inches above the floor. Or we do some wall math and try to center everything in the space between the top of the sofa and the ceiling. I'm not sure either of those is the best way to go about hanging art. To me, it's more important for your art to communicate with and be close to the piece it's hanging above. If hanging art close to the furniture feels too low in relationship to the ceiling, that means either you need to find a taller piece to go in that space, or you need to hang a coordinating piece of art above it to achieve the height you desire.

Now, a few words about that gallery wall you're dying to create. Gallery walls are one of the most complex design challenges you'll ever undertake. If picking out a rug takes an elementary design education, a gallery wall takes a doctorate. Too many of us have been doing gallery walls all wrong, creating them as a last resort to compensate for not having sufficiently large art instead of creating them on purpose with purpose.

When we use items that are too small, we soon realize they look awkward because they don't fill the space correctly (they violate the two-thirds rule), so we add more and more small pieces to make up for it. The result? We end up with a haphazard mess of scatter art because we started off with a piece of art that wasn't the right size for the space. Then we complicate matters by hanging the pieces too far apart from each other and too high in relation to what's below.

To create a gallery wall on purpose *with* purpose, begin by hanging a few large items close together. Remember, we want the wall art to look like it's in a happy relationship with whatever it's hanging above and with what's hanging next to it.

Because we know the correct order to put a room together, choosing the right art for the right space is going to be easier than it's ever been. We've already created some limitations for ourselves (which is helpful!) just by where we've decided to place everything else in the room. Prioritizing your walls helps to banish overwhelm, allowing you to focus on one wall at a time. Don't move on until a wall feels right. But also, don't feel like you need to fill every wall with art.

## WALL SABBATHS

A wall sabbath is the white space, the empty space, that surrounds anything on your walls. Empty space is the secret to using your walls in the best way possible, and is just as important as filled space.

Aim for having some empty wall space in every room. In life, we need margin so we can take a breath, rest, and focus on what's most important. In our home, we need white space for the same reasons. It helps us to visually take a breath, rest, and focus on what's most important. It's hard to do that when every wall is full of stuff.

TOP Art that is too small for a space makes us want to fill up the space by hanging more art.

MIDDLE When we add extra art simply to fill space, we end up with an accidental gallery wall.

BOTTOM Instead of accidentally creating a gallery wall, start fresh with a large, risky signature piece of art. You'll end up getting more style with less stuff.

Empty space is the secret to using your walls in the best way possible, and is just as important as filled space.

Art becomes more of a focus when there's some breathing room around it. Think about divine proportion and the two-thirds rule; they allow for white space around art. Don't force every wall in your room to hold art. Sometimes a wall full of windows, especially if those windows have drapes, is beautiful without adding art. Sometimes an empty wall is more beautiful and peaceful than a gallery wall.

Although some walls add calm by being empty, most walls are begging to hold some art. Please don't be afraid to make a nail hole. I once had a wall that had eighty-three nail holes in it (a gallery wall gone bad). It took less than twenty minutes to fill the holes right before we moved out. Totally worth it.

You could have the same room layout with the same furniture, rugs, and drapes as your next-door neighbor, but you can completely change what a room looks like with the treatments, colors, and art you put on the walls. This is where your creativity and personal style can really come through without your having to invest in an expensive statement piece like a pink sofa. When it comes to wall art, consider the phrase "less but better." Better doesn't mean more expensive, but it might mean larger, riskier, out-of-your-comfort-zone pieces. Once you have your walls the way you want them, your room is 95 percent finished!

Style is to see
beauty in modesty.

—ANDRÉ PUTMAN

CHAPTER 9

# ACCESSORIES

Styling the Finishing Touches

Finally!

This chapter covers the decorating task we always try to start with. We think if we could just group our accessories together in a cute way, then our rooms would look pulled together and complete. If only we knew how to style a room with accessories! I have one thing to say about that:

Lipstick on a pig.

The Stuff Manager goes straight to work putting the sofa on the longest wall, hanging random art above it, and grouping accessories on every surface. Then she looks back at all her hard work and wonders why the room doesn't feel finished. So she panics and runs out and buys more of the wrong stuff—trendy accessories, pillows, and set-arounds—thinking they will help cozy up the room.

But you're not a Stuff Manager. You're a Home Curator, a Cozy Minimalist who knows a better way. That's why you've taken the time and made the effort to first quiet the room and place your furniture in a way that works best for you and your family. With the right furniture in the right place, a large rug, drapes hung correctly, well-placed lighting, and the right size art, you've already created a cozy room.

You're a Home Curator,
a Cozy Minimalist who
knows a better way.

Congratulations! Your space is 95 percent finished! Once you get to this point, if you followed all the steps, you'll realize that you need only a few accessories for that finishing touch. If you are an accessory addict like I was, you might be shocked at how much you've been relying on accessories to add style to your room. But when you complete the steps in order, you will add so much style as you go that the pressure is off when it comes to adding in some pretty accessories.

Now you are ready to face that pile of accessories you packed away back in chapter 5 so we can create some lovely vignettes with what you already have. But first, we need to designate our surfaces.

## IT'S TIME TO DESIGNATE!

I used to think the purpose of an accessory was to fill those dreaded empty spaces. Yee-haw, pretty space fillers! Give me the latest and greatest, and I'll fill every surface to within an inch of my life! To me, an empty surface was simply an unfinished area I had yet to fill with cute stuff.

Now I realize that empty surfaces are just as valuable and just as hard-working as filled spaces. Not only do I value some empty space; I actually plan for it, and you can too.

> Empty surfaces are just as valuable and just as hardworking as filled spaces.

### DESIGNATED EMPTY SURFACES

Our kitchen table is our breakfast table, is our dining room table, is our puzzle table, is our bill paying table, is our report card signing table, is our cat relaxing table. Needless to say, that table works hard for our family and cats all day long.

Unlike the first half of my years decorating a home, I no longer have decorative stuff that permanently resides on my kitchen table. I like to have some surfaces—such as our hardworking table—that are left empty so we can use them throughout the day without having to repeatedly find a temporary home for a bunch of cute, decorative stuff.

I also have nothing decorative that permanently resides on my kitchen island because I need every square inch of my counters for cooking, organizing, folding laundry, and procrastinating at putting other stuff away. In order to have some order in my life, I don't keep decorative objects on the kitchen island. Does this mean my island is always empty? Nope, it's actually one of the most used surfaces in my house. But when it's not in use, it's gloriously empty. Doesn't an empty kitchen counter seem like the most extravagant luxury?

I find a lot of beauty in my kitchen island when it's completely empty, but it's also beautiful in a different way when it's full of the evidence of life. There really is something glorious about a kitchen counter stacked with dirty dishes, an empty wine bottle, and leftover cookies. We call that a beautiful mess, and it definitely has its place. Why? Because it is an indicator that you are fully living your life. It's good and okay to have some messes around from time to time. The point isn't for some surfaces to always be empty; it's for all surfaces to work hard for our family.

Our table and kitchen counters are what I call "Designated Empty Surfaces (Yippee!)" or DESYs for short. This is an expression of the minimalist part of cozy. One of the best gifts I ever gave myself was to assign some surfaces in our home as DESYs. Instead of seeing every clear surface as a space to be filled,

I now see our empty kitchen counters as finished and ready to serve. It doesn't mean the surface is always empty; it just means I don't use the space for permanent décor or accessories.

Having a few DESYs has served our family so well that even though I'm far from being a tidy-and-clean freak, when our kitchen island is full of stuff, I'm extra motivated to clear it off because I know having it empty makes me happy. In the past, I always had to drag myself into the kitchen to clean it up. Now that I know a clean counter has such a magical effect on me, I'm eager to get our kitchen counter cleared off and gloriously empty.

Look at your own room and choose your DESY. Your Designated Empty Surface (Yippee!) will serve you best if it's often in use, like the coffee table or the dining table. Ideally, you want to choose a DESY that will make your life easier by being empty in its natural state. If you find yourself constantly moving décor off a surface so you can use it in different ways, that surface might be telling you that it wants to be a DESY.

Just as I have designated empty spaces, I also have some spaces designated for décor in every room of our house that I style with accessories. At the moment, those places are our mantel, the side table next to our kitchen table, the console table in the hall, my dresser, and a display shelf in our back entryway.

Aim for one surface per room that is designated for décor. This is a protected area that serves your family by displaying beautiful, meaningful accessories. This should be a space that's away from the center of daily action. Fireplace mantels, sofa tables, consoles, sideboards, and dressers are perfect for displaying styled accessories.

# VIGNETTES

Everything that sits out in your home is décor. Just look around.

The gym bag that's been sitting by the back door for days? Décor.

The box of stuff for the thrift store that's been in the corner of the family room for three weeks? *Bam!* That's décor.

The stack of magazines you keep meaning to go through that date back to last year, all falling over on that shelf on the coffee table? *Poof!* You are decorating with old magazines.

Vignettes are a way to decorate with purpose. Think of the grouping of décor on a mantel: that's a vignette. Usually vignettes involve a little art, maybe a lamp, and a few meaningful accessories combined in a way that looks pretty and balanced. When you get a vignette looking the way you want, you naturally won't want to wreck it with gym bags, giveaway piles, and magazines. I love the perks of becoming a CoMi!

## BRING OUT THE ACCESSORIES

It's time to take your accessory pile for this room out of storage. Before you get started making vignettes on your designated surfaces, I want you to take a good look at your accessories.

Anything that has a negative emotion attached to it, like guilt or shame,

ABOVE Enjoy the little things, but don't try to create vignettes with lots of items smaller than a pineapple.

should be moved to a separate pile so you can get rid of it. We aren't gonna use this stuff. Life's too short to surround yourself with stuff that makes you feel like a bad person. Also, remove anything that you just don't like or don't want to use. Your pile of accessories should all be stuff that you actually really love to look at. Once you eliminate some things, I'm assuming you'll still have other things left to work with, such as baskets, vases, framed photos, decorative trays, candlesticks, plants, and other trinkets. Now you have some meaningful beauty that you love to look at to work into your space.

## LOOK FOR THE STYLE FACTORS

Most of us know how to choose accessories for our home that we love; the problem comes when it's time to group them together in a way that looks pretty. When it comes to grouping accessories, it's all about finding balance. I try to keep in mind four style factors when curating my vignettes. If I can use accessories that have these style factors, then I know I'm going to achieve visual balance.

The right combination of style factors creates visual presence. There are many style factors, but I want to focus on four that make the biggest impact. Everyone knows you can add impact with a pop of color, but color can take you only so far. In addition to color, there are four things you want to be mindful of in every room and every vignette: scale, shape, mass, and texture. Knowing these style factors will help you create a balanced vignette.

1. SCALE. Scale is the size of something in relationship to the things around it. As Cozy Minimalists whose goal is more style with less stuff, we know that one large item usually serves us better than a bunch of tiny items. One large item has more presence and impact than a bunch of smalls. And it costs less most of the time. Look at your accessory pile. What's the average size of your decorative objects? Most of us collect lots of smalls, which is anything smaller than a pineapple. But it's helpful to have some larger objects to work with as well. Look back at your Pinterest board, and focus on the scale of the tchotchkes in the rooms. Most homes with a balanced design look use large-scale objects that have a bigger impact on the room. Do you see it? Using only small pieces is the number one mistake people make when vignetting. Next time you are shopping for something like a vase, and there are small, medium, and large versions, get the large one.

Everything that sits out in your home
is décor. Just look around.

2. SHAPE. Look at an object's silhouette, and consider the shape. I like to have three groups represented in my decorative arsenal: straight lines, curved lines, and organic shapes. Most of us have lots of straight lines in our homes to begin with: floor tiles, windows, and bricks. We often have decorative stuff with lots of right angles and straight lines, such as boxes and frames and books.

You also want to bring in some softness with curves. A gourd lamp, sphere shapes in artwork, and rounded objects help to round out a room.

Finally, you want some organic shapes like plants, branches, or brass animals. Even a decorative throw can be an organic shape. Look back at the Pinterest board you created, this time with an eye for shapes. My guess is you'll find straight lines, curvy lines, and organic shapes in many of the photos.

LEFT Organic-shape decor

RIGHT Curved-shape decor

ABOVE Straight-edge decor

ABOVE Textured decor (roughage)

When it comes to grouping
accessories, it's all about
finding balance.

3. TEXTURE. Texture is roughage for a room. Think about it: when everything in a space is shiny, smooth, and slick, your eye just slides right by. When we fail to incorporate texture, most rooms end up with visual diarrhea. A room full of slick stuff has a bad case of diarrhea. These rooms can be full of beautiful things, but something about them feels weak or off, which is a lack of texture. We need something to stop our eyes. We need texture that will act like roughage. Better to have more texture than less. We can add texture with things like rough wood, woven baskets, chunky blankets, and nubby fabrics—anything that isn't smooth or slick. To get a balanced look, we want both smooth pieces and rough textures in a room.

4. MASS. Mass is the visual weight of your stuff. This is why a room full of stuff can still feel what we here in the South call "nekkid." Or why a room with three huge items can feel heavy and clunky. This is not about how much something actually weighs but about how much visual space it takes up. Think about airy ironwork, glass, and thin metal objects like baskets and skinny lamps. I sometimes shy away from these types of things, not because they are bad or wrong, but because as a Cozy Minimalist, I want to squeeze the most style out of the least amount of stuff.

Open, airy, visually lightweight pieces aren't usually the best choice for providing visual oomph. However, sometimes I need to quietly sneak something into a room without it taking up too much visual space—then I go right for this lightweight stuff. Items with visual weight have more of a voice in a room, more of a presence, which means they add more style. And yet they might take up the same amount of physical space.

These four style factors will help you look at the accessories in your accessory pile objectively, based on their physical properties alone. You already like everything in your pile; now you just need to decide how to use it. This is how you view your stuff as a Chief Home Curator: for what it has to offer visually, which then allows you to decide what looks good together. Now, let's talk about where to start.

## CATEGORIZE YOUR ACCESSORIES

A Chief Home Curator approaches vignettes with purpose. When she looks at her stuff, she is able to detach from her emotions (she already loves what she has) so she can focus on style factors. Then she looks at her stuff and arranges it into categories so she can style a balanced vignette and get the finished look she wants. First, go ahead and separate out any pillows or throws. Right now, we are going to focus on accessories we can use for vignettes.

There are four categories you'll want to pull from to create vignettes in your home:

1. **Focal pieces:** large focal pieces that demand attention, usually extra art or a large-scale accessory like an architectural salvage piece
2. **Containers:** vases, baskets, bowls, pottery, planters, boxes
3. **Plants:** Every cozy home needs some kind of plant. I love real plants, but if you insist on fake, I understand. Plants and greenery bring so much life to a room and fill in empty spaces like magic. I promise, it's worth figuring out which kind you can keep alive.
4. **Decorative objects and meaningful beauty:** figurines, mementos, framed photos, kids' creations, candlesticks, collections

Go ahead and sort your accessories into these four piles. If something fits in more than one category, that's fine. You just want to make sure you have at least a few items in each category so you can put together balanced vignettes. If you don't yet have any plants, consider buying one. Or at least go out into your yard and cut some branches off of something green. Don't worry too much if you don't have many focal pieces; the art you already hung on your wall can act as the focal piece. And just because you grouped your items into four categories doesn't mean you have to use them all. A Cozy Minimalist prides herself in knowing when to stop. If you love your mantel with only a focal piece on it, great—stop there!

Now that you know how to categorize your stuff, it's time to get your vignette on!

## HOW TO STYLE A MANTEL VIGNETTE

Even though I don't like formulas, I'm going to give you a simple vignette formula. Not because it's the only way to vignette, but because it's a great way to start to notice the relationship between objects and become aware of what looks good together and why. Once you get this simple formula down,

LEFT How I styled my mantel as a Stuff Manager. I added all of my favorite small things until there was no room left. More stuff, but less style.

RIGHT How I style my mantel as a Cozy Minimalist. I use large, interesting, meaningful pieces incorporating the style factors that result in beauty and balance. More style and, amazingly, less stuff!

# A Chief Home Curator approaches vignettes with purpose.

*give and it will be given to you. A good measure pressed down shaken together and running over will be poured into your lap. For with the measure you use it will be measured to you.* LUKE 6:38

you can change it up and add more or fewer items and experiment with what looks good together. Then you'll be a pro at vignetting!

Let's start with your mantel. Mantels are a great way to start learning how to vignette because they are relatively small surfaces and usually don't need to serve a purpose other than being decorative. Overall, you don't have that much room to fill up, so if you have a mantel, I want you to start there. Even if you don't have a mantel, you'll still benefit from reading this section because all the same principles apply to the other surfaces you want to vignette—the console in the hall, the dresser in your bedroom, the sideboard in your family room, etc.

Your goal is to incorporate the four style factors into any vignette you create, while keeping in mind the overall goal we CoMis have for our home: more style, less stuff. This means you'll add presence and style using items that have scale, shape, mass, and texture. This results in a balanced vignette that incorporates meaningful beauty using your art and accessories. I'm assuming you already have colors you like represented in your accessories, so we aren't even going to talk about that. We're just going to focus on how to make your things look good together.

ASSESS YOUR MANTEL. If you happen to have hung a piece of art over your mantel in the last chapter, that's great! Now I want you to take it down just for a minute so you can see your mantel again. Look at your empty mantel like the Home Curator that you are. Does it already have any of our four style factors—scale, shape, mass, or texture? I bet it does! If your fireplace is brick, you already have lots of straight lines. Check that off the list. My mantel is a large chunk of rustic wood sitting on a painted brick fireplace. So without adding anything, I've already got texture and lots of straight edges happening. Isn't this fun?

CHOOSE THE FOCAL PIECE. Once you take inventory of what your mantel already provides, look back at your wall art and your accessories, and consider shopping the house if you need to. You are looking for a large-scale focal piece to put above the mantel. Most likely you already did this in the last chapter. This is going to be the focal point of your vignette. Remember divine proportion and the two-thirds rule? Ideally, you want your focal piece to fill about two-thirds of your mantel space.

As Cozy Minimalists, we want to get the most style out of the least amount of stuff. So we will gravitate toward large-scale items, and when we create a vignette, we know we need a focal point. That's why we want that one large-scale focal piece. If your focal piece is too small, you'll feel the need to fill in the extra space with extra stuff, which defeats our entire purpose.

Once you find your focal piece, lean it, hang it, or get it up on your mantel somehow. Now make a mental note of which of the four style qualities it possesses. I'm making you choose something with a large scale, so you've already got that. Does it also have mass? Texture? What shapes are happening? There is no wrong answer here; you just want to identify which of the four style factors aren't represented between the mantel and the focal piece so you can try to pull in the missing factors with one of the next objects you choose. Isn't this fun? It's just making the next best decision. You are so doing this!

My focal piece is a large black-and-white canvas. It's got scale, visual mass, straight lines, and because of the word "Relax," I've even got some round and organic lines going on! Because my mantel already has straight lines, I know I want to shy away from adding more lines if possible. And remember, my mantel already has texture from the wood, so that's covered too. I've covered all my style factors in just a few pieces!

CHOOSE A CONTAINER. Next, I want you to look back at your accessories, or shop the house again if you need to, and add a container. Choose a container that provides any style factor your mantel may be lacking. If you are

lacking mass, look for a chunky container like a thick wood planter. If your mantel is starting to look like it has diarrhea, add some roughage with a textured basket. If your focal piece is a round or oval mirror, you might want to add a vase with some straight edges. For my mantel, I shopped the house and found a two-tone round vase with a little texture.

ADD SOME GREEN. Your container is lonely and wants a friend. If you have a large container, you can plop in a potted plant. If you used a tall, thin container, consider adding in a few tall branches. In the summer, look for branches from the yard. In the winter, find a place to cut some evergreens. Grocery store flowers add a lot of color for just a few dollars. And of course, if you need to go for something fake so you don't have to think about it, do that. Add your greenery/plant, and look at that—you've got your organic shape! Isn't this fun? Do not underestimate the power of a plant in your room. Once you start using greens and plants, you'll wonder how you ever lived without them.

For my mantel, I cut a few stems from a plant in another room. I allowed the leaves in the vase to cover a little of the canvas. Placement is crucial here.

You want your pieces to feel like a little family, so don't separate them like they are marching in a parade. Try overlapping a piece or two; it makes the vignette look purposeful.

STOP AND CONSIDER. Dear CoMi, this is where we get all caught up and don't know where to stop. I want you to step back and look at your curated mantel with the fabulous, large-scale focal piece, the pretty container, and the greenery or plant. If you did this right, you love each piece that you've chosen so far. And each piece brings a lot of your own personal style to the room because you chose pieces that you like which also represent the four style factors. Way to go!

Does your mantel truly need more stuff to get the style you love? Only you can answer this question. But I want you to know that it's been so freeing to me and my accessory-loving self to give myself permission to stop over-accessorizing. There is so much beauty and freedom in enough. My mantel is finished with just a vase containing some leaves and a gloriously beautiful canvas. I no longer need the trio of candlesticks, the stacked books, or the layers of art to have a pretty mantel. I just needed to add a few well-chosen pieces, and I'm able to have less stuff but still have a stunning mantel that's just my style. That's our goal. More style, less stuff.

DECORATIVE OBJECTS. We're all about freedom here, and if your mantel feels too empty for your style, this is where you can add some decorative objects. You might have a higher need for some cozy abundance on your mantel, and that's fine. Remember, it's not about counting your stuff; it's about recognizing when you have enough to get the look you are after. Consider the style factors—if you've got a lot of straight lines happening, balance them with some curves, or vice versa.

The ideal Cozy Minimalist vignette incorporates just enough beauty to get the style you are looking for. If you combine the four types of pieces with your mantel itself, and incorporate each of the four style factors—shape, scale, texture, and mass—you are virtually guaranteed to create a balanced, beautiful vignette.

Now you can take these steps and apply them to any surface you want to vignette. If you are creating a vignette on a dresser, start with your focal piece and then, if needed, work a lamp in as you apply the style factors.

Creating vignettes gets easier over time. It also teaches you how to shop specifically for items you need. There have been many times my shopping list was ultra-specific when I needed a tall, angular, textured vase or a round, shiny decorative object. Doesn't that make shopping easier than aimlessly looking for "cute mantel décor"?

## COLLECTIONS

A bowling ball collection is more difficult to display than a diamond ring collection, but both can be featured if you love them enough to work them into your home. Remember, just because you've always had something isn't reason enough to keep it. A collection that meant something to someone else doesn't have to become a burden to you.

If you have a collection you love, treat it well, display it, enjoy it, and by all means, show it off all together in one spot. A collection displayed on different surfaces and in different rooms takes away from the overall impact. My friend Meg collects vintage globes, and they look amazing all perched on top of her kitchen cabinets. They'd have a lot less impact if they were spread out around her house. Collections want to be displayed together.

## FAMILY PHOTOS

If you have a bunch of framed photos, you should definitely incorporate your favorite photos into your home. I used to sprinkle photos all over my house on every surface, and that's fine, but lately, I've wanted to play up our pretty family photos and feature them. Now I'm planning for a family photo wall in our soon-to-be-family-room in the basement.

Consider grouping all your framed photos together to make a bigger impact. I love to see a table in a corner filled with framed family photos. Or maybe it's time to protect all those original photos in an album and instead choose a favorite photo to have enlarged into a focal piece so it gets the attention it deserves. Decide which room benefits the most from family photos and focus them all in one space to really highlight your precious photos. Usually, a hallway or family room is an ideal place for photos. A CoMi sees the value of playing up and displaying her family photos in a way that gives them the focus they deserve.

The ideal Cozy Minimalist vignette incorporates just enough beauty to get the style you are looking for.

## PILLOWS AND THROWS

While we are on the topic of accessories, let's chat about creating a little beauty on the chairs, sofa, and bed. Pillows and throws aren't purely decorative; they actually help us get cozy and stay comfy on the furniture in our rooms, and they add both beauty and function to a room.

As Cozy Minimalists, we might opt for the sofa or chair with the neutral fabric because we are sure it will stand the test of time. But pillows and throws allow even the most neutral-loving CoMi to take a calculated, returnable risk. Pillows are our chance to experiment with scale (hint: get the bigger pillow), texture, color, and pattern. I like to look for feather-stuffed pillows because they don't lose their shape. Extra points if you find pillows with removable, washable covers.

Throws are a great way to add more color and texture to an upholstered piece. Think about your pillow and throw combinations like an outfit. It's not about matching things; it's about putting things together that go together.

## WHEN BUYING A LAMP

Remember how I suggested back in chapter 7 that you to wait to purchase a new lamp until you read this chapter? Now that you are familiar with the style factors, ideally, you'll want a lamp that not only adds light to a room but also adds style. As Cozy Minimalists, we want the things in our home to be multipurpose. When it comes to lamps, look for varieties with bases that bring some large scale and mass to a room.

## ABOUT THAT SEASONAL DÉCOR

If you are like me, you long for your home to reflect the season. I like this about us.

A Stuff Manager relies heavily on store-bought seasonal and holiday décor to nod to the season. She collects as much seasonal décor as possible, layers it on most surfaces, and then hopes she has enough energy to organize it and pack it all up in its coordinating seasonal bin at the end of the season.

A CoMi understands that visual décor is just one small way to embrace a season.

Think about how you experience each season outside of your home. You experience the world through your five senses. We smell the grass after a spring rain, we hear the crunch of autumn leaves under our boots, we feel the warmth of the sun in the summer and the biting chill of the winter wind. We taste the autumn cider, the Easter ham, the perfectly ripe watermelon, and the champagne toast, and we instantly recognize each season, no home décor necessary.

When it comes to incorporating the seasons into our home, a Cozy Minimalist caters to all five senses instead of focusing only on the visual.

Décor isn't the only way to set the mood in a home. You can create a seasonal feel simply with the foods you serve (bonus points because you are creating a seasonal scent at the same time). Add your favorite candle or essential oil, and the scents that fill your house throughout the year will be the strongest memory trigger your family will ever experience.

A Cozy Minimalist caters to all five
senses instead of focusing only
on the visual.

Sprinkle in some sounds from open windows or a curated playlist, and you are really creating a seasonal atmosphere. Consider the sense of touch and how to incorporate that into your home throughout the year as well. Heavily textured throws and flannel sheets in the cooler months, a sprinkler or blow-up pool for the kiddos to cool down in the summer—these are all ways we create a home that can be enjoyed in every season.

Seasons and moods can also be enhanced by the things we provide in our homes for people to do. Stacks of books and puzzles and a supply of firewood make it easier to cozy up by the fireplace. Marshmallows, skewers, bubbles, and sparklers naturally invite us to go outside and enjoy a summer night. These are the things we want to provide in our homes to welcome the season. These things help us actually enjoy and experience each season and have nothing to do with décor.

Instead of looking for seasonal décor, first look for seasonal equipment or supplies. These accompaniments will help your family enjoy each season to its fullest, as well as incorporate the five senses.

Once you consider the other four senses, then add a little visual décor.

Instead of purchasing décor that can be used only for a season and then has to be organized away, consider natural seasonal items you can find inexpensively or even free. Pinecones, branches, pumpkins, sunflowers, shells, and evergreens are a great place to start.

When it comes to décor that helps highlight a season, it's great to have serving dishes in various sizes that can double as decorative containers and trays, candlesticks and candles, and a few special pillows and throws that feel more summery or wintery.

I shy away from anything that figuratively or literally announces the season it belongs to. I can use a mercury glass candlestick all year around, unless someone printed the words "Merry Christmas" on it. Ideally, we want to invest in decorative items that can work all through the year. Change out the pumpkin with the evergreen branch, and the candlestick still looks cozy.

## LEFTOVER ACCESSORIES

Now that you are a Cozy Minimalist, there's a good chance you'll feel like your room is finished well before you use all the accessories that you removed from your room when you started this process. That's normal and a good thing! It can be helpful to keep a box of favorite decorative objects around until you've worked through every room of your house. That way, if you need a container or extra photo frame, you don't have to replace something you gave away last week. Still, while it can be helpful to keep that box of accessories around while you cozy-minimalize the rest of your house, it can defeat the entire purpose if you start squirreling away all sorts of décor forever, just in case. This is what truly separates the Stuff Managers from the Chief Home Curators. You are now a Cozy Minimalist!

He who knows he has
enough is rich.

—LAO TZU

# CHAPTER 10

# ENOUGH

Better Than More

Look around the room you've been working on. Your furniture is set up in a way that serves your family. You've decided on big cozifiers like a rug and drapes, and you have some well-placed lamps and purposeful lighting. If the room needed painting, you painted. If it needed some placeholders or temporary fixes, you addressed them. You've got just enough art on the walls, some surfaces with pretty vignettes, and some empty surfaces just waiting for you to use them to the fullest. Your room is filled with just the right amount of stuff, which means—happy surprise—cleaning it is not the chore it used to be!

Congratulations! Your room is done. I'm not saying it's perfect. I'm not saying it's completely finished for the rest of time, because you'll continue to change and your needs will change, and it's your job as Chief Home Curator to make sure the room continues to serve the changing needs of your people. You did it, maybe for the first time ever. Allow yourself to enjoy a room in your house that is done. This means you can finally stop thinking about, fretting over, shopping for, and concerning yourself with this room. You did your part.

## REAPPLY AND REPEAT

Now that one room is done and you are enjoying the simple cozy space, you are going to crave the same thing for all of the other rooms in your house. And now that you've done it once, it's going to be so much easier to cozy-minimalize your other spaces. Be patient, and remember to work on only one room at a time. As you repeat the process for each room in your home, you'll find it easier to make confident decisions.

From time to time, your finished rooms may start to feel crowded or like they need a touch-up. About once a year, I feel like my family room has some stuff buildup. I usually get this feeling after Christmas or during the spring. If and when any of your rooms start to feel this way, there's a simple fix: quiet the room. Most likely, a scaled-down version of quieting that focuses on accessories will do the trick. Move all the accessories into a holding area for a few hours. Wipe down all your surfaces, and take a mental inventory of everything still in the room. If it's still working and serving your family well, then great. If something feels off or is no longer working, go back to the corresponding chapter and work through it again. Once you are ready, evaluate your accessories and work through chapter 9 again. If you don't need to make major changes, you should be able to reset your room in a few hours.

As you repeat the process for each room in your home, you'll find it easier to make confident decisions.

## BACKWARDS DECLUTTERING

Once your rooms are done, you still aren't quite finished. I'm guessing you have somewhere between a little and a ton of leftover stuff. You've got furniture and accessories that you no longer need. And now that your home is finished, you can finally be sure about what you do and don't need. Yes, I tricked you! Suddenly, the things you no longer need are obvious and getting in the way of your intentional home. It's time to let go!

For years, I kept lots of extra furniture and décor around (stored in closets and stuffed into corners) because my home never felt finished. And if my rooms weren't done, then I wasn't able to make an informed decision about what I needed to keep and what I needed to let go. No wonder I was stuck.

Once I approached my house as a Cozy Minimalist, I became addicted to having just enough in our home. The same will happen to you.

Once you finish your home and see how freeing it is to live with just the

A Cozy Minimalist doesn't
keep stuff out of guilt or sunk costs.
Be graceful and forgive yourself.

right amount of stuff, you'll never want to go back to piling stuff, no matter how cute it is. Suddenly, you'll be free to get rid of the extra stuff.

This is the best part—you'll have a pretty, finished home that you love, and you'll no longer have to wonder if you need to keep stuff around to finish it. It should be easy to part with that extra stuff because you don't want to junk up those quiet, beautiful rooms. You proved to yourself that you don't need to be surrounded by so much stuff, and now you can let go of the excess.

It's okay to get rid of stuff. A Cozy Minimalist doesn't keep stuff out of guilt or sunk costs. Deciding to keep something just because getting rid of it feels wasteful is Stuff Manager logic. Wastefulness is keeping something you don't need and won't use, and if that's the case, the money was wasted way back when you purchased it. The money you spent isn't recouped because you decide to keep what you spent it on. Be graceful and forgive yourself. What's done is done. Now give it away to a home where it can be used and loved.

After I cozy-minimalized my home, I had a basement full of cute, unused stuff. I took two carloads to the local church thrift store, I gave one carload to a friend, and I sold the rest. My advice? Get rid of your excess stuff in the way that brings you the least amount of stress and the most joy. When it comes to having a garage sale, consider what Joshua Becker has to say: "The simple benefits of generosity far outweigh the financial rewards of most garage sales."

## ENOUGH

One of the best parts of Cozy Minimalism is this odd sensation you begin to experience—one that most people never allow themselves to feel. It's called "enough."

Many people never know they are allowed to say they have enough. It almost seems un-American. Enough doesn't mean everything is perfect; it simply means you have enough because you've met a goal. Whether in your home, at work, in your closet, on your dinner plate, or in your schedule, you get to say, "That's enough." You not only get to say enough, you have to say it. A big part of our job as grown-ups is to recognize when we have enough and call it out. We don't say we have enough because we don't know how to get more; we say "enough" because we don't want or need more. We've decided to end the quest for more because there's something we want more than more.

More for the sake of more is just as empty as less for the sake of less. The race to the bottom is just as meaningless as the race to the top because the focus is still on the race. Constantly focusing on how little we can live with is just as much of a distraction as focusing on how much more we can acquire. Minimalism and materialism aren't all that different when the focus is all about how much we have. It's not about stuff at all. It's about changing our focus.

Once you realize you have enough, you're free to see how much extra you have—and then you'll want to start sharing it. This is what happens when you finally realize you've had enough all along, and you just didn't know what to do with it. When we realize we have enough, we're freed to give the rest away. For those of us who have always felt a call to making home, feeling like

Enough doesn't mean everything is perfect; it simply means you have enough because you've met a goal.

our house is done and ready for people releases us from obsessing about our home. We can finally move on.

In the years since I CoMi'd my house, I've discovered that when I have less, I am able to contribute more. Buying less stuff and having less stuff means I have more time and money to contribute to other things like nonprofits, our church, and people we believe in. Less is the gift to myself that keeps on giving.

## HOW TO KNOW WHEN A ROOM FEELS RIGHT

The goal is to get your home in a place where you can forget about it. Yep. I wrote two entire books about home to help you stop thinking about your house! I guess my job here is done.

You'll know you've arrived when you invite someone over and the first thing that crosses your mind isn't, *I wonder what they'll think of my home.* Instead, your first thought is about your guest: *I wonder if they are gluten free and what I can cook for them for dinner.* Or *I wonder how she's feeling*

You'll know your home is in a good place when you go from thinking about how to make it look better to thinking about how to make it serve better.

*since her daughter just left for college.* Or *Where are those toys we kept around? Maybe our guests' kids can play with them while we visit.* No, silly, this isn't because you've come to accept your ugly home or because you are finally past the whole "beauty thing." May we *never* get past that—we love beauty! In fact, you value beauty so much, you've already committed to doing the hard work necessary to create a home you love. And now you can stop fretting over it!

Over time, I've found my method of getting ready for guests is much less focused on my house and how it looks (which is a fancy way of saying I'm less me-focused), and much more focused on my heart and whether I'm in a place to truly listen to, connect with, and be attentive to my guests. This is a strange phenomenon, and it didn't happen overnight. I used to fret over every detail of my house, rearrange vignettes, buy fresh flowers, and try to envision my home from the perspective of a new guest. However, as I focused on creating a place that serves me and others, that represents my family, that I find beautiful, and that isn't overflowing with stuff, I began to think less and less about my house when I had people over. *Instead, I began to think about the people.* And that feels right. You'll know your home is in a good place when you go from thinking about how to make it look better to thinking about how to make it serve better.

Being a Cozy Minimalist takes more thought than being a sold-out minimalist or a sold-out maximalist. You are committing to a lifelong practice of paying attention and evaluating your home based on your needs and the needs of the people you love. You know your home serves you best when it's somewhere in the center of that tension between peaceful simplicity and cozy abundance. Now go love your family and friends in your Cozy Minimalist home.

# ACKNOWLEDGMENTS

It's tempting to list everyone I know here, because truly there is a connection to how everyone you know plays a role in what you create. But in the spirit of minimalism, I want to thank:

- God, the original designer, the first maker, the relentless beauty hunter.
- Chad, Landis, Cademon, and Gavin, the men who put up with me at home.
- Emily, baby sister, soul-stirring writer, sounding board, sanity keeper.
- Mom and Dad, who are endlessly supportive.
- The Cozy Minimalist community, who trusted a girl without a design degree to teach them how to design their own homes with purpose.
- The 2016 Tuscan Writers Retreat-ers, listeners who shared lots of truth and wine.
- Jenni, retreat leader, friend, and agent.
- Caroline and Greg, the kind of friends everyone always hopes to have.
- Tsh, Kendra, Megan, Lisa, Jessica, Logan, Angela, Mandi, Niki, Emily, and Anne for friendships that last and make a difference.
- Carolyn: it's unnatural and probably unprofessional how much I adore my editor.
- Alicia, who lets me be an INTJ, Enneagram 5.
- Brian and Julie, who believed in this idea when it was an ugly baby.
- Caleb, who taught me how to use a camera that wasn't also a phone.
- Sean and Christie, John and Marcy, Tell and Karen, Caleb and Elaine, and Kurt and Melissa.
- Lindsay, whose creativity constantly leaves me speechless.
- Edie, my favorite maximalist and the reason I will never be a full-on minimalist.

# COZY MINIMALIST
# HOME RECIPE

START with super-comfy primary seating, ideally in a style that has a name.

ADD some secondary seating that's comfy enough.

SPRINKLE around surfaces and storage.

LAYER with a large rug.

COMBINE floor-to-ceiling drapes.

INCORPORATE lighting and lamps with presence.

SURROUND with just enough large wall art.

ADD a pinch of accessorized vignettes.

FILL with people; add love.

ENJOY your Cozy Minimalist space.

# COZY MINIMALIST
# MANIFESTO

WE BELIEVE that home exists to serve people, not the other way around.

WE BELIEVE it is a sacred calling to be watchful about what comes into our home and purposeful about what goes out.

WE BELIEVE unique style always trumps trends, and that an uncomplicated home is a blessing to everyone who enters it.

WE BELIEVE that empty spaces are just as important, beautiful, and useful as filled spaces.

WE BELIEVE home is an ever-shifting combination of grace, coziness, abundance, simplicity, form, and function.

WE BELIEVE that it doesn't have to be perfect to be beautiful.

WE BELIEVE that it doesn't have to be cluttered to be cozy, and that it doesn't have to be modern to be minimal.

WE BELIEVE we truly can have more style with less stuff.

# FAMILY ROOM
## BEFORE AND AFTER

Here are before and after photos of my family room,
contrasting when I styled it as a Stuff Manager
and when I styled it like a Cozy Minimalist.

LEFT The decorative items I used in the family room before I cozy-minimalized the space. Notice the small scale, lack of presence, and lifelessness.

RIGHT The decorative items I used to cozy-minimalize the space. Notice how I used fewer, but larger scale, items and lots of plants.

# The Nesting Place

## It Doesn't Have to Be Perfect to Be Beautiful

*Myquillyn Smith, The Nester*

Perfection is overrated.

Popular blogger and self-taught decorator Myquillyn Smith (The Nester) is all about embracing reality—especially when it comes to decorating a home bursting with boys, pets, and all the unpredictable messes of life.

In *The Nesting Place*, Myquillyn shares the secrets of decorating for real people—and it has nothing to do with creating a flawless look to wow your guests. It has everything to do with embracing the natural imperfection and chaos of daily living.

Drawing on her years of experience as a decorator, Myquillyn will show you how to simply and creatively tailor your home to reflect you and your unique style—without breaking the bank or stressing over comparisons. Full of easy tips, simple steps, and practical advice, *The Nesting Place* will give you the courage to take risks with your home and transform it into a place that's inviting and warm for family and friends.

There is beauty in the lived-in and loved-on and just-about-used-up, Myquillyn says, and welcoming that imperfection wholeheartedly just might be the most freeing thing you'll ever do.